It's another winner from the CGP lab...

There are only three ways to make sure you're fully prepared for the new Grade 9-1 GCSE Combined Science exams — practice, practice and practice.

That's why we've packed this brilliant CGP book with realistic exam-style questions for every topic, and we've got all the practicals covered too.

And since you'll be tested on a wide range of topics in the real exams, we've also included sections of mixed questions for Biology, Chemistry and Physics!

CGP — still the best! ☺

Our sole aim here at CGP is to produce the highest quality books — carefully written, immaculately presented and dangerously close to being funny.

Then we work our socks off to get them out to you — at the cheapest possible prices.

Contents

☑ Use the tick boxes to check off the topics you've completed.

Published by CGP

Editors:

Katie Braid, Jane Ellingham, Robin Flello, Emily Forsberg, Emily Garrett, Sharon Keeley-Holden, Emily Howe, Christopher Lindle, Duncan Lindsay, Ciara McGlade, Rachael Rogers, Frances Rooney, Camilla Simson, Hayley Thompson, Charlotte Whiteley and Sarah Williams.

Contributors:

Sophie Anderson, Ian Davis, Alison Dennis, Mark A. Edwards, Bethan Parry, Alison Popperwell and Chris Workman.

ISBN: 978 1 78294 486 7

With thanks to Susan Alexander, Charlotte Burrows, Mark A. Edwards, Mary Falkner, Katherine Faudemer, Rachel Kordan, Sarah Pattison, and Jamie Sinclair for the proofreading.

With thanks to Ana Pungartnik for the copyright research.

Data in the graph on page 138 showing the change in atmospheric CO_2 concentration provided by Carbon Cycle and Greenhouse Gases group, 325 Broadway R/CSD, Boulder, CO 80305 (http://esrl.noaa.gov/gmd/ccgg/)

Table on page 206 contains public sector information licensed under the Open Government Licence v3.0. http://www.nationalarchives.gov.uk/doc/open-government-licence/version/3/

Clipart from Corel®
Illustrations by: Sandy Gardner Artist, email sandy@sandygardner.co.uk
Printed by Elanders Ltd, Newcastle upon Tyne

Based on the classic CGP style created by Richard Parsons.

How to Use This Book

- Hold the book <u>upright</u>, approximately <u>50 cm</u> from your face, ensuring that the text looks like <u>this</u>, not <u>sıɥʇ</u>.
- In case of emergency, press the two halves of the book together <u>firmly</u> in order to close.
- Before attempting to use this book, read the following <u>safety information</u>:

The questions are arranged into sub-topics, so you can get exam practice on exactly the bit of your course that you want.

You'll have done some 'required practical activities' as part of your course. You could be asked about any of them in your exams. Whenever one of the required practical activities crops up in this book, it's marked up like this.

There are warm-up questions for the trickier sub-topics, to ease you in and get you thinking along the right lines.

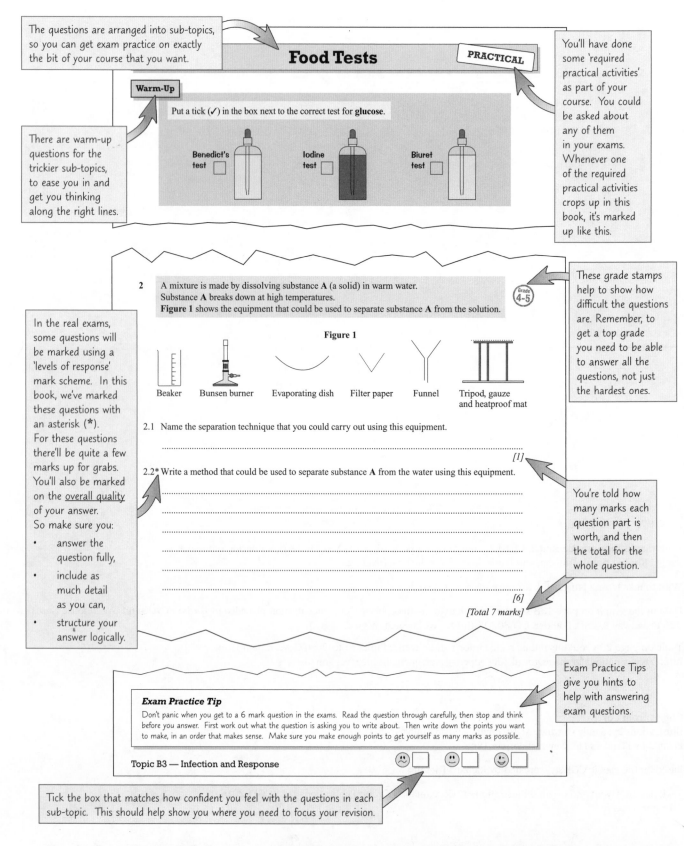

Food Tests

PRACTICAL

Warm-Up

Put a tick (✓) in the box next to the correct test for **glucose**.

Benedict's test ☐   Iodine test ☐   Biuret test ☐

2   A mixture is made by dissolving substance **A** (a solid) in warm water.
Substance **A** breaks down at high temperatures.
Figure 1 shows the equipment that could be used to separate substance **A** from the solution.

Grade 4-5

These grade stamps help to show how difficult the questions are. Remember, to get a top grade you need to be able to answer all the questions, not just the hardest ones.

Figure 1

Beaker   Bunsen burner   Evaporating dish   Filter paper   Funnel   Tripod, gauze and heatproof mat

2.1 Name the separation technique that you could carry out using this equipment.

....
[1]

2.2* Write a method that could be used to separate substance **A** from the water using this equipment.

....

....

....

....

....

....
[6]
[Total 7 marks]

In the real exams, some questions will be marked using a 'levels of response' mark scheme. In this book, we've marked these questions with an asterisk (*). For these questions there'll be quite a few marks up for grabs. You'll also be marked on the <u>overall quality</u> of your answer. So make sure you:

- answer the question fully,
- include as much detail as you can,
- structure your answer logically.

You're told how many marks each question part is worth, and then the total for the whole question.

Exam Practice Tip
Don't panic when you get to a 6 mark question in the exams. Read the question through carefully, then stop and think before you answer. First work out what the question is asking you to write about. Then write down the points you want to make, in an order that makes sense. Make sure you make enough points to get yourself as many marks as possible.

Exam Practice Tips give you hints to help with answering exam questions.

Topic B3 — Infection and Response   ☹ ☐ ☺ ☐ ☺ ☐

Tick the box that matches how confident you feel with the questions in each sub-topic. This should help show you where you need to focus your revision.

- There's also a Physics Equations List at the back of this book — you'll be given these equations in your exam. You can look up equations on this list to help you answer some of the physics questions in this book.

How to Use This Book

Cells

Complete the table to show whether each statement is **true** for eukaryotic cells or prokaryotic cells. Tick **one** box in each row.

Statement	Eukaryotic cells	Prokaryotic cells
These cells have a nucleus.	✓	✓
These are the smallest type of cell.		✓
These cells can be bacteria.		✓

1 **Figure 1** shows a diagram of an animal cell. *(Grade 3-4)*

Figure 1

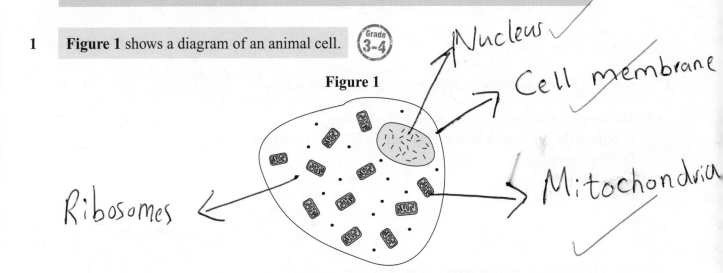

Nucleus ✓
Cell membrane
Mitochondria ✓
Ribosomes

1.1 Label the cell membrane, the nucleus and a mitochondrion on **Figure 1**.

[3]

1.2 Give the function of each part of the cell on **Figure 1**.

Cell membrane ~~Sto~~ Controls the entry and exit of substances inside cell.

Mitochondria Releases energy from respiration ✓ aerobic

Nucleus Contains the Blueprint of the cell. ✓ Controls genetic material

[3]

1.3 Name **two** other subcellular structures that can be found in an animal cell.

1. Golgi apparatus ✓   Cytoplasm

2. Ribosomes

[2]

1.4 Give **one** reason why the diagram in **Figure 1** does not represent a plant cell.

Plant cells are protected by a cell wall, where as animal cells aren't.

[1]

[Total 9 marks]

Microscopy

1 A student observed blood cells under a microscope.
A scale drawing of one of the cells is shown in **Figure 1**.

Grade 1-3

Figure 1

A

In **Figure 1**, A is the image width.

1.1 Measure the length of A with a ruler. .... ~~24~~ 23 .... mm

[1]

1.2 The real width of the cell is 0.012 mm.
What is the magnification of the image in **Figure 1**?
Use the formula:

$$\text{magnification} = \frac{\text{image size}}{\text{real size}}$$

$$\frac{23}{0.012} = 250$$

$$X2000$$

magnification = × ......250.....×

[1]

[Total 2 marks]

2 A plant cell is magnified 1000 times using a light microscope.

Grade 3-4

2.1 The length of the image of the plant cell is 10 mm.
Calculate the real length of one plant cell in millimetres (mm).
Use the formula:

$$\text{real size} = \frac{\text{image size}}{\text{magnification}}$$

$$\text{real size} = \frac{10}{1000} =$$

......0.01...... mm ✓

[1]

2.2 What is the length of one plant cell in micrometres (μm)?

$$1mm = 1000\,\mu m \implies \cancel{10mm \times 1000}\;\; \overset{0.1mm \times 1000}{\underset{=10,000 = 10\mu m}{}}\;\; 10,000 ....$$ μm ✗

[1]

2.3 How do magnification and resolution compare between electron and light microscopes?
Tick **one** box.

Magnification and resolution are the same for electron microscopes and light microscopes. ☑

Electron microscopes have a lower magnification and resolution than light microscopes. ☐

Electron microscopes have a higher magnification and resolution than light microscopes. ☑

[1]

2.4 Give **one** way in which electron microscopy has increased understanding of subcellular structures.

?

......More subcellular structures can be seen.......

[1]

[Total 4 marks]

> **Exam Practice Tip**
> Make sure you know how to convert one unit to another. To go from a bigger unit to a smaller unit (for example, from millimetres to micrometres) your calculation should be a <u>multiplication</u>. To go from a smaller unit to a bigger unit (e.g. from micrometres to millimetres) your calculation should be a <u>division</u>.

3

More on Microscopy PRACTICAL

1 A student wants to use a light microscope to view a sample of onion cells. (Grade 4-5)

1.1 The student adds a drop of iodine stain to her sample.
Which statement best describes why a stain might be used to view a sample of tissue?
Tick **one** box.

To make the specimen easier to cut. ☐

To make the specimen easier to see. ☑ ✓

To prevent air bubbles forming. ☐

To help the cover slip stick to the slide. ☐

[1]

Figure 1 shows a diagram of the light microscope that the student plans to use.

1.2 The three different objective lenses are labelled in **Figure 1**
with their magnification.
Which lens should the student select first when viewing her cells?

__X4 Objective lens__ ✓

[1]

× 10
× 40
× 4

1.3 After she has selected the objective lens, she looks down
the eyepiece and uses the adjustment knobs.
Describe the purpose of the adjustment knobs.

__The adjustment knob adjusts__
__the focus of the image, so__
__that it is made clearer.__ → Move stage to bring sample into focus.

[1]

1.4 The student wants to see the cells at a greater magnification.
Describe the steps that she should take.

← Use adjustment knobs • __The student should first ʄ/ use the 4x__
__objective lens and adjust it to find a clear image.__
__• Then the student needs to increase the objective__
__lens to a greater one (x10) to see a more magnified image.__ [2]

1.5 After she has viewed the cells, she wants to produce a scientific drawing of them.
Her teacher has told her to use smooth lines to draw the structures she can see.
Give **two** other ways in which she can make sure she produces an accurate and useful drawing. Label important feature

1. __Draw whilst looking through the microscope__ X

2. __Include a title__

[2]

[Total 7 marks]

☹ ☐   ☺ ☐   ☺ ☐

Topic B1 — Cell Biology

Cell Differentiation and Specialisation

Complete the sentence below. Use a word from the box.

| specialisation | differentiation | adaptation |

The process by which cells change to carry out specific functions is called ...*differentia-tion*

1 Specialised cells have different structures.
This allows them to carry out different functions.

Draw straight lines to match up each type of plant cell with its structure and function.

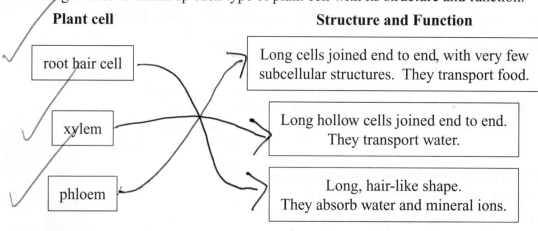

Plant cell

root hair cell

xylem

phloem

Structure and Function

Long cells joined end to end, with very few subcellular structures. They transport food.

Long hollow cells joined end to end. They transport water.

Long, hair-like shape. They absorb water and mineral ions.

[Total 2 marks]

2 A sperm cell is specialised for its function. Grade 3-4

2.1 What is the function of a sperm cell?
~~A fu~~ The function of a sperm cell is to fuse with an ova to create a zygote. *carry male DNA to the egg* *[1]*

Figure 1 shows a sperm cell.

Figure 1

tail
mitochondria

2.2 How does the sperm cell's **tail** help it to carry out its function?
The tail helps to propel the sperm cell towards the ova.
[1]

2.3 Describe how **mitochondria** help the sperm cell to carry out its function.
Mitochondria releases energy, which is used by the sperm cell for movement.
[1]

[Total 3 marks]

Chromosomes and Mitosis

1   **Figure 1** shows a cell during the cell cycle. Grade 4-5

Figure 1

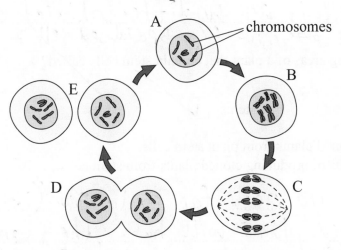

chromosomes

A
E
B
D
C

1.1 Cell **A** is preparing to divide. What is happening to the chromosomes in cell A?
Tick **one** box.

The chromosomes are dividing. ☐

The chromosomes are being copied. ☑

The chromosomes are getting longer. ☐

[1]

1.2 What else is happening in cell **A**?
Tick **one** box.

The number of mitochondria is increasing. ☐   No. of mitochondria is increasing

The number of ribosomes is decreasing. ☐   ✗

The nucleus is dividing. ☑

[1]

1.3 Describe what is happening to cell **D**.

• In cell D, the cell is dividing into two cells
with double the number of Chromosomes

[2]

1.4 How do the two cells produced at stage **E** compare to cell **A**?
Tick **one** box.

They are genetically different. ☐

They are genetically similar. ☐

They are genetically identical. ☑

[1]

[Total 5 marks]

       Topic B1 — Cell Biology

6

Stem Cells

1 Stem cells can be found in the growing areas of plants. *(Grade 4-5)*

1.1 What is a stem cell?

A stem cell is an undifferentiated cell that can become ~~an~~ into any specialised cell in the body. [1]

1.2 What are the growing areas of a plant that contain stem cells called?
Tick **one** box.

cloning zones ☐   meristems ☑   leaves ☐   mesophyll layers ☐

[1]

1.3 You can produce cloned plants from plant stem cells.
Describe **two** benefits of producing cloned plants from stem cells.

→ *quicker/cheaper*

1. *There is no need for pollination (i.e. only one gender needed)*
2. *The cloned plant will have the same desirable characteristics as the parent plant.*

[2]

[Total 4 marks]

2 The technique shown in **Figure 1** could be used to produce cells for some medical treatments. *(Grade 4-5)*

Figure 1

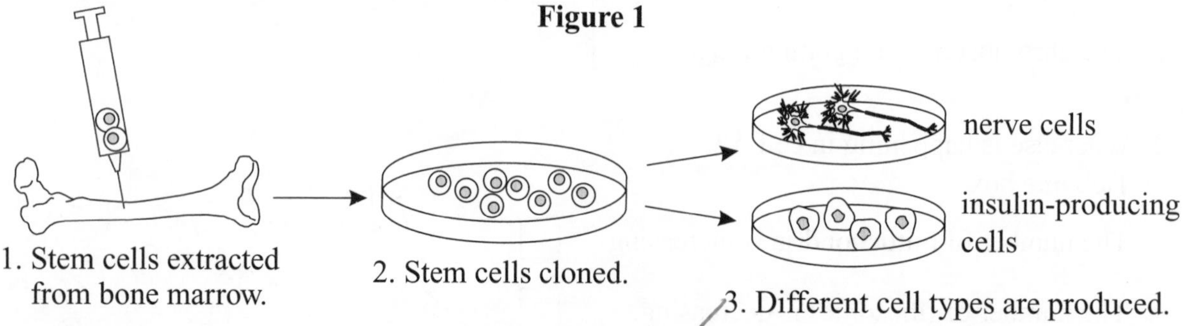

1. Stem cells extracted from bone marrow.
2. Stem cells cloned.
3. Different cell types are produced.

nerve cells

insulin-producing cells

2.1 Name **one** medical condition that may be helped by treatment using stem cells.

Macular degeneration

[1]

2.2 Apart from bone marrow, give **one** other source of stem cells for medical treatments.

Embryos from humans

[1]

2.3 Suggest **one** reason why some people may be **against** using the source of stem cells you named in **2.2**.

Can be used for chosing child characteristics → *designer babies*

[1]

2.4 Give **one** potential **risk** of using stem cells in medical treatments.

Potential risk stem cells can be infected with a virus that may pass onto a patient-

[1]

[Total 4 marks]

Topic B1 — Cell Biology

☹ ☐   ☺ ☐   ☺ ☐

Diffusion

1 **Figure 1** shows glucose molecules diffusing through a cell membrane.

Figure 1

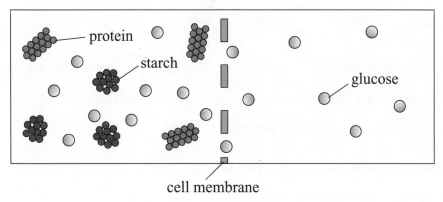

1.1 In which direction will most of the glucose molecules be moving?
Draw an arrow on **Figure 1** to show your answer.

[1]

1.2 Why can't the protein molecules in **Figure 1** diffuse through the membrane?

....

[1]

1.3 As glucose diffuses from one side of the membrane to the other,
its concentration gradient decreases. Which statement is correct?
Tick **one** box.

A decrease in the concentration gradient will have no effect on the rate of diffusion. ☐

A decrease in the concentration gradient will increase the rate of diffusion. ☐

A decrease in the concentration gradient will decrease the rate of diffusion. ☐

[1]

[Total 3 marks]

2 A student adds a drop of ink to a glass of cold water.

2.1 What will the student observe happening to the drop of ink?
Explain your answer.

....

....

....

[2]

2.2 How might the observation differ if the ink was added to a glass of warm water?

....

[1]

[Total 3 marks]

Topic B1 — Cell Biology

Osmosis

1 Some molecules move by osmosis.

1.1 Use the words in the box to complete the following definition of osmosis:

water	more	less	sugar

Osmosis is the movement of .... molecules across a partially

permeable membrane from a .... concentrated solution

to a .... concentrated solution.

[3]

1.2 In which of these is osmosis occurring? Tick **one** box.

A plant is absorbing water from the soil. ☐

Sugar is being taken up into the blood from the gut. ☐

Water is evaporating from a leaf. ☐

Oxygen is entering the blood from the lungs. ☐

[1]

[Total 4 marks]

PRACTICAL

2 A student did an experiment to see the effect of different salt solutions on pieces of potato.

• He cut five equal-sized chips from a raw potato and measured the mass of each chip.
• Each chip was placed in a beaker containing a different concentration of salt solution.
• The mass of each chip was measured again after 24 hours. The results are shown in **Table 1**.

Table 1

Beaker	1	2	3	4	5
Mass of potato chip at start of experiment (g)	5.70	5.73	5.71	5.75	5.77
Mass of potato chip after 24 hours (g)	6.71	6.58	6.27	5.46	4.63
Percentage change in mass of potato chip (%)	17.7	?	9.81	−5.04	−19.8

2.1 Calculate the percentage change in mass for the potato chip in beaker 2.

.... %

[2]

2.2 Explain why the chips in beakers 4 and 5 lost mass.

....

....

[2]

[Total 4 marks]

Topic B1 — Cell Biology

Active Transport

1 Glucose molecules can be absorbed from the gut into the blood by active transport. *(Grade 4-5)*

1.1 What is active transport?

....

....

[1]

1.2 How are glucose molecules used inside cells?

....

[1]

1.3 Which of these statements about active transport is correct?
Tick **one** box.

It's a type of diffusion. ☐

It can only occur down a concentration gradient. ☐

It needs energy from respiration. ☐

It needs energy from photosynthesis. ☐

[1]

[Total 3 marks]

2 Plants absorb mineral ions from the soil by active transport. *(Grade 4-5)*

2.1 Why do plants need mineral ions?

....

[1]

2.2 Why do plants need to use active transport to absorb mineral ions from the soil?

....

....

[2]

2.3 State **two** ways in which active transport differs from diffusion.

1. ....

2. ....

[2]

[Total 5 marks]

Exam Practice Tip

Diffusion, osmosis and active transport are tricky ideas to get your head around, but it's really important that you do. Make a list of the important facts about each process and learn it. It might help you to remember that active transport works in pretty much the opposite way to diffusion.

 ☐   ☐   ☐

Topic B1 — Cell Biology

Exchanging Substances

Place the following organisms in order according to their surface area to volume ratio. Number the boxes 1 to 3, with 1 being the smallest and 3 being the largest.

☐ Tiger   ☐ Bacterium   ☐ Blue whale

1 The cube in **Figure 1** represents a small cell. `Grade 3-4`

Figure 1

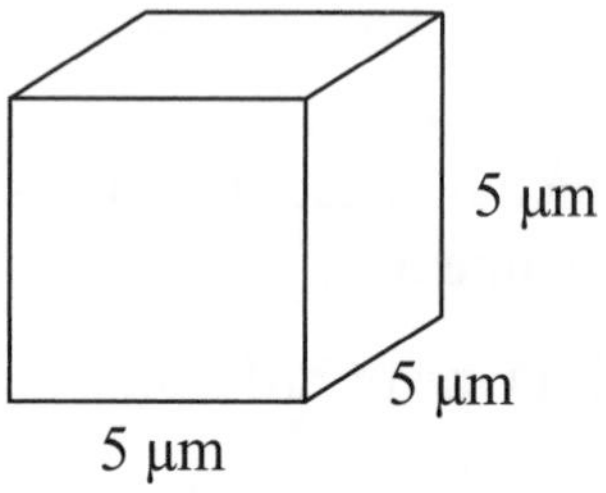

5 µm
5 µm
5 µm

1.1 What is the volume of the cube? Tick **one** box.

5 µm³ ☐   15 µm³ ☐

125 µm³ ☐   150 µm³ ☐

[1]

1.2 What is the surface area of the cube? Tick **one** box.

5 µm² ☐   15 µm² ☐   125 µm² ☐   150 µm² ☐

[1]

1.3 Another cell has a surface area of 24 µm². It has a volume of 8 µm³. What is its surface area to volume ratio? Tick **one** box.

3:1 ☐   2:1 ☐   1:3 ☐   1:2 ☐

[1]

[Total 3 marks]

2 **Figure 2** shows the relative sizes of an Arctic hare and a polar bear.   Both animals live in cold, snowy conditions. `Grade 4-5`

Figure 2

polar bear

Arctic hare

Having a large surface area to volume ratio increases the rate at which an organism loses heat.

Which of the organisms in **Figure 2** is more likely to have difficulty keeping warm in the Arctic? Explain your answer.

....

....

....

....

[Total 3 marks]

Topic B1 — Cell Biology

☹ ☐   ☺ ☐   ☺ ☐

More on Exchanging Substances

Warm-Up

Which of these are adaptations of a gas exchange surface in animals?
One has been circled for you. Circle **three** more.

a thin membrane   a good blood supply   a thick membrane

being flat   (a large surface area)   being ventilated

---

1 Digested food is absorbed into the blood from the small intestine. *(Grade 1-3)*
Which of the following statements is correct? Tick **one** box.

Villi decrease the blood supply to the small intestine. ☐

A single layer of surface cells increases the surface area of the small intestine. ☐

Villi increase the surface area of the small intestine. ☐

[Total 1 mark]

2 **Figure 1** shows an alveolus in the lungs. *(Grade 3-4)*

Figure 1

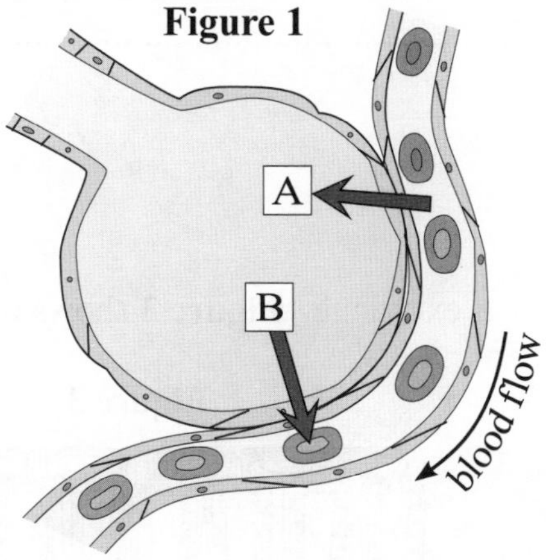

2.1 Name gases A and B.

A ....

B ....

[2]

2.2 By what process do these gases move across the membrane?

....

[1]

2.3 State which feature of the lungs gives:

gases a short distance to move ....

a large surface area ....

[2]

[Total 5 marks]

Topic B1 — Cell Biology

3 **Figure 2** shows a diagram of a fish gill. This is a gas exchange surface.

Figure 2

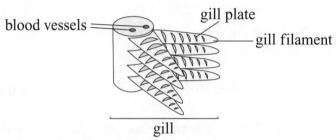

3.1 Describe the movement of gases in a fish gill.

....

....

[2]

3.2 The gill filaments and gill plates have the same purpose. Suggest what this purpose is.

....

[1]

3.3 Give **one** other feature of a fish gill.
    Explain how it makes gas exchange more efficient.

....

....

[2]

[Total 5 marks]

4* Leaves are adapted for gas exchange. **Figure 3** shows the cross-section of a leaf.

Figure 3

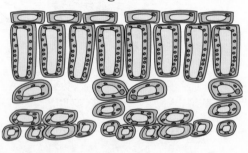

Explain how a leaf is adapted for efficient gas exchange.

....

....

....

....

....

[Total 4 marks]

Topic B1 — Cell Biology

Cell Organisation

Number the boxes 1 to 4 to put the body components in order of size.
Number 1 should be the smallest component. Number 4 should be the largest component.

☐ Organ system   ☐ Tissue   ☐ Cell   ☐ Organ

1   **Figure 1** is a diagram of the human digestive system.
Three organs are labelled **X**, **Y** and **Z**.

Grade **4-5**

Figure 1

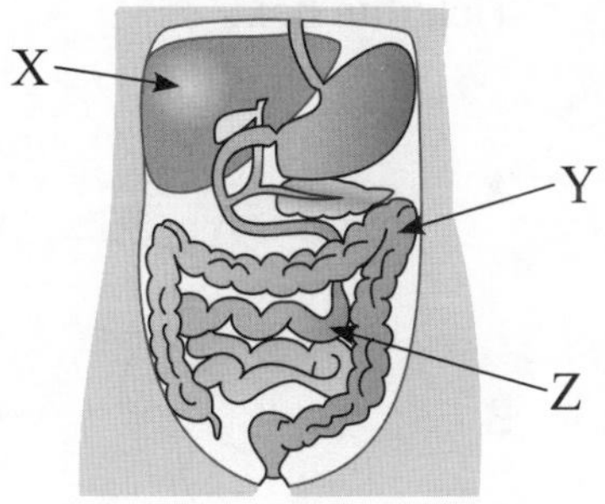

X

Y

Z

1.1   Draw **one** line to match each letter below to the
name of the organ it represents in **Figure 1**.

Letter

☐ X

☐ Y

☐ Z

Name of organ

liver

small intestine

large intestine

stomach

[3]

1.2   What is an organ?

....

....

[1]

1.3   The digestive system is an organ system.
What is meant by the term 'organ system'?

....

....

[1]

1.4   Organ systems contain multiple types of tissue.
What is a tissue?

....

....

[1]

1.5   What is the role of the digestive system?

....

[1]

[Total 7 marks]

 ☐   ☐   ☐

Enzymes

1 The shape of an enzyme is important for its job. **Figure 1** shows an enzyme.

Grade 1-3

Figure 1

1.1 Name the part of the enzyme labelled **X** in **Figure 1**.

....
[1]

X →

1.2 The enzyme in **Figure 1** catalyses a reaction that breaks apart a substrate.
Which reaction, **A**, **B** or **C**, will the enzyme in **Figure 1** catalyse?
Tick **one** box.

A ☐

B ☐

C ☐

[1]

[Total 2 marks]

2 A reaction is catalysed by an enzyme. **Figure 2** shows how temperature affects the rate of this reaction.

Grade 4-5

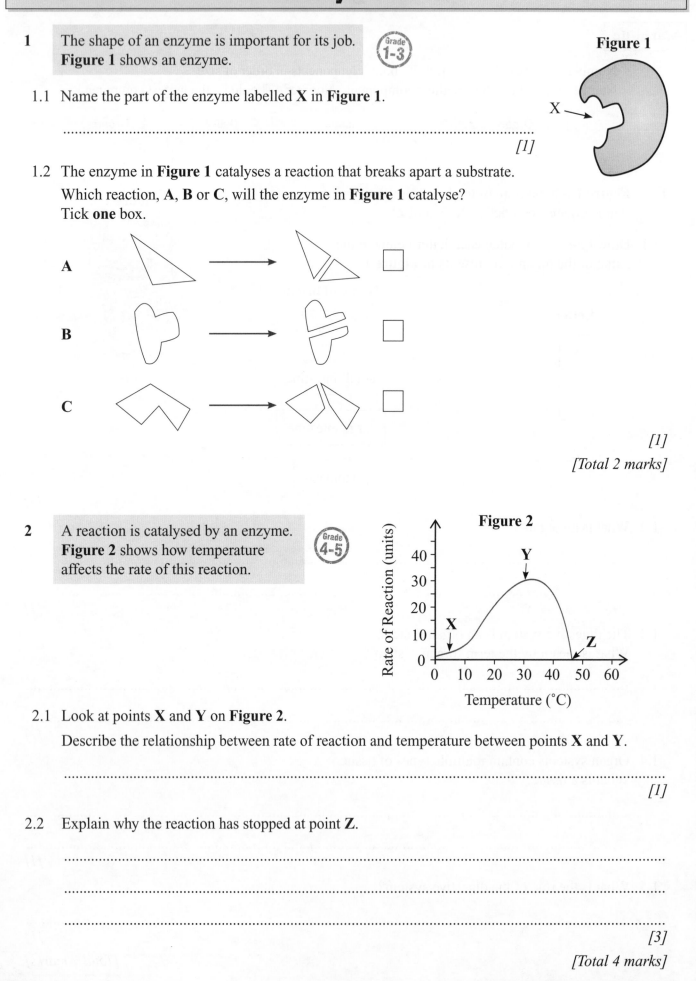

Figure 2

2.1 Look at points **X** and **Y** on **Figure 2**.

Describe the relationship between rate of reaction and temperature between points **X** and **Y**.

....
[1]

2.2 Explain why the reaction has stopped at point **Z**.

....

....

....
[3]

[Total 4 marks]

Investigating Enzymatic Reactions [PRACTICAL]

1   Amylase is an enzyme.   (Grade 3-4)

1.1   Which of the following statements about amylase is correct?
Tick **one** box.

Amylase joins sugar molecules together to make starch.   ☐

Amylase helps to break down sugar into starch.   ☐

Amylase helps to break down starch into amino acids.   ☐

Amylase helps to break down starch into sugar.   ☐

[1]

Iodine solution can be used in investigations into the activity of amylase.

1.2   Describe the colour change that takes place when iodine solution
is added to a solution containing starch.

....

....

[2]

[Total 3 marks]

2   A student investigated the effect of pH on amylase activity.   (Grade 4-5)

He added amylase solution to three test tubes, **X**, **Y** and **Z**.
Each test tube contained: •   a starch solution.
•   a buffer solution with a different pH.

2.1   Give **one** way that the student could control the temperature in the test tubes.

....

[1]

Table 1 shows how long it took for the reaction in each test tube to finish.

Table 1

Test tube	Time (s)	Rate of reaction
X	110	9.1
Y	40	....
Z	190	....

2.2   Complete **Table 1** to show the rate of the reactions in test tubes **Y** and **Z**.

Use the equation: $\text{Rate} = \dfrac{1000}{\text{time}}$

Give each of your answers to 2 significant figures.

[2]

2.3   What are the units for the 'Rate of reaction' column in **Table 1**? Tick **one** box.

second (s)   ☐   per second (s^{-1})   ☐   time (t)   ☐

[1]

[Total 4 marks]

 ☐   ☐   ☐

Topic B2 — Organisation

Enzymes and Digestion

1 Enzymes are involved in digestion in the human body. **Grade 1-3**

1.1 Draw **one or more** lines from each type of molecule to the products of its digestion.

Type of molecule

carbohydrate

lipid

protein

Products of digestion

amino acids

sugars

glycerol

fatty acids

[4]

1.2 Lipases are digestive enzymes.
What type of molecule do lipases break down? Tick **one** box.

Carbohydrates ☐   Lipids ☐   Proteins ☐

[1]

1.3 Give **two** places in the body that produce lipases.

1. ....   2. ....

[2]

[Total 7 marks]

2 Bile is used in the digestion of fats by enzymes. **Grade 3-4**

2.1 Complete the sentences below.
Use words from the box.

| gall bladder | small intestine | alkaline | acidic |
| liver | neutralises | emulsifies | |

Bile is produced by the .... It is stored in the ....

It has an .... pH, so it .... acid from the stomach.

It also .... fats.

[5]

2.2 Fats are broken down into tiny droplets before being digested by enzymes.
Why does this make digestion by enzymes happen faster?

....

....

[1]

[Total 6 marks]

Exam Practice Tip

The molecule that an enzyme breaks down is usually in its name, e.g. <u>carbohydr</u>ases break down <u>carbohydr</u>ates.
Knowing that should make learning the names of most of these enzymes, and what they do, much easier.

Topic B2 — Organisation   ☐   ☐   ☺ ☐

Food Tests

Put a tick (✓) in the box next to the correct test for **glucose**.

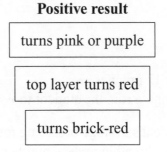

Benedict's test ☐   Iodine test ☐   Biuret test ☐

---

1 Many food tests involve a colour change. Grade 1-3

Draw **one** line to match each of the following tests to its positive result.

Positive result

Test	
Benedict's	
Biuret	

turns pink or purple

top layer turns red

turns brick-red

[Total 2 marks]

2* A student has a sample of cooked butter beans. Grade 4-5
He wants to find out if the beans contain protein.

Describe how the student could:
- prepare a sample of the beans for testing.
- test for protein in his prepared sample.

....

....

....

....

....

....

....

....

....

....

....

[Total 6 marks]

Topic B2 — Organisation

The Lungs

1 **Figure 1** shows the structure of the lungs in humans. (Grade 1-3)

Figure 1

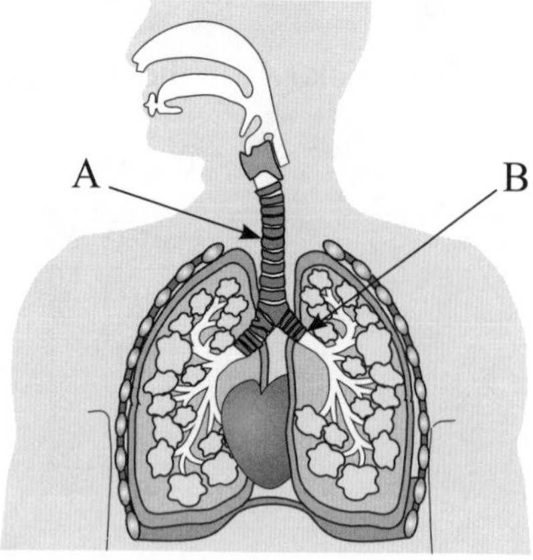

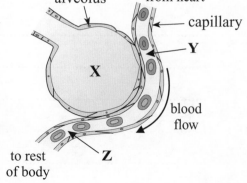

1.1 What is structure **A** on **Figure 1**?
Tick **one** box.

bronchus ☐

trachea ☐

alveolus ☐

[1]

1.2 What is structure **B** on **Figure 1**?
Tick **one** box.

bronchus ☐   trachea ☐   alveolus ☐

[1]

[Total 2 marks]

2 A student ran for 12 minutes.
During this 12 minute run, the student took 495 breaths. (Grade 3-4)

Calculate the student's average breathing rate.
Use the equation: breathing rate = number of breaths ÷ number of minutes

Give your answer to 3 significant figures.

.... breaths per minute

[Total 2 marks]

3 **Figure 2** shows an alveolus surrounded by a capillary.
Table 1 shows the relative concentrations of oxygen
and carbon dioxide at positions **X**, **Y** and **Z** in **Figure 2**. (Grade 4-5)

Complete **Table 1** by writing **high** or **low** in the empty cells.

Figure 2

Table 1

	Oxygen concentration	Carbon dioxide concentration
X	High	Low
Y	Low	....
Z	....	....

[Total 3 marks]

Circulatory System — The Heart

1 **Figure 1** shows a diagram of the heart. (Grade 1-3)

Figure 1

X   pulmonary vein

1.1 What is the part of the heart labelled **X**? Tick **one** box.

vena cava ☐

pulmonary artery ☐

aorta ☐

[1]

The arrows on **Figure 1** show the direction of blood flow through the **left side** of the heart.

1.2 Which of the following answers should be used to complete the sentence?
Write the correct letter, **A**, **B** or **C** in the box below.

A   vena cava

B   pulmonary artery

C   aorta

The left ventricle pumps blood through the ☐ to cells all over the body.

[1]

1.3 Draw arrows on **Figure 1** to show the direction of blood flow through the **right side** of the heart.

[1]

[Total 3 marks]

2 The heart has a pacemaker. (Grade 3-4)

2.1 Which of these statements about the pacemaker is true?
Tick **one** box.

It is found in the left atrium. ☐   It keeps blood flowing in the right direction. ☐

It controls the resting heart rate. ☐   It supplies the heart muscle with blood. ☐

[1]

2.2 Suggest why someone might need to be given an artificial pacemaker.

....

[1]

[Total 2 marks]

3 Explain why the human circulatory system is described as a 'double circulatory system'. (Grade 4-5)

....

....

....

....

....

[Total 3 marks]

 ☐   ☐   ☐

Topic B2 — Organisation

Circulatory System — Blood Vessels

1 **Figure 1** shows the three types of blood vessel.

Figure 1

  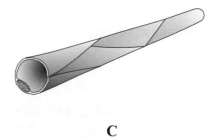

A   B   C

Which of these blood vessels, **A**, **B** or **C**, is an artery?

Write your answer in the box. ☐

Give a reason for your answer.

....

....

[Total 2 marks]

2 Different types of blood vessel have different structures and functions.

2.1 Complete **Table 1** to show whether each feature is part of a capillary, an artery or a vein.
Put a tick in each row.

Table 1

Feature	Capillary	Artery	Vein
Elastic fibres in blood vessel walls			
Large lumen			
Thin walls, with gaps between the cells			
Valves			

[3]

2.2 Describe the function of capillaries.

....

....

[2]

2.3 Explain why arteries have a different structure to veins.

....

....

....

[2]

[Total 7 marks]

Circulatory System — Blood

1 The blood has several different parts. **Figure 1** shows a white blood cell.

Grade 1-3

Figure 1

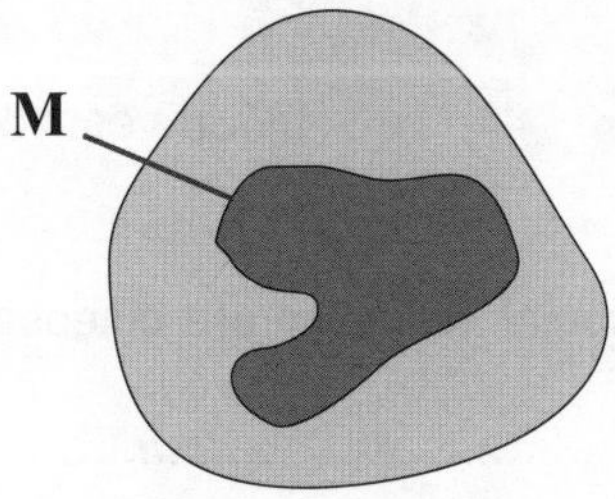

1.1 What is structure **M** on **Figure 1**?
Tick **one** box.

cytoplasm ☐

cell membrane ☐

nucleus ☐

[1]

1.2 The different parts of the blood are carried in a liquid.
What is this liquid called?
Tick **one** box.

plasma ☐   cell sap ☐   urine ☐   bile ☐

[1]

1.3 Which of the following parts of the blood is responsible for clotting?
Tick **one** box.

white blood cells ☐   red blood cells ☐   platelets ☐   antibodies ☐

[1]

[Total 3 marks]

2 Red blood cells carry oxygen around the body. **Figure 2** shows the shape of a red blood cell.

Grade 3-4

Figure 2

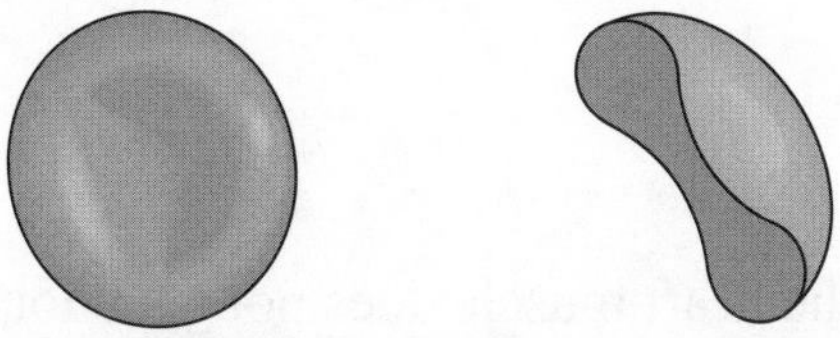

View from above   Cut through view

2.1 Describe how a red blood cell's shape helps it to carry out its function.

....

[1]

2.2 Red blood cells don't have a nucleus.
How does this help them to carry out their function?

....

[1]

2.3 Give **one** more feature of red blood cells that help them to carry out their function.

....

[1]

[Total 3 marks]

 ☐   ☐   ☐

Topic B2 — Organisation

Cardiovascular Disease

Fill in the gaps to complete the following sentence. Choose **two** of the words below.

lungs   blood vessels   heart   legs

Cardiovascular diseases are diseases of the ....

and the ....

---

1 Statins are drugs that can be used to prevent cardiovascular diseases. **Grade 3-4**

1.1 What do statins do?
Tick **one** box.

They lower the blood cholesterol level. ☐

They increase the blood cholesterol level. ☐

They remove all cholesterol from the blood. ☐

[1]

1.2 Give **one** disadvantage of using statins to prevent cardiovascular diseases.

....

....

[1]

[Total 2 marks]

---

2 Heart attacks happen when the heart muscle does not get enough oxygen. **Grade 4-5**

2.1 Explain how **stents** prevent heart attacks from happening.

....

....

....

[2]

2.2 A doctor is advising a patient about having a stent fitted.
Give **one** risk that the doctor is likely to tell the patient about.

....

....

[1]

[Total 3 marks]

More on Cardiovascular Disease

1 A man has a leaky heart valve. (Grade 4-5)

1.1 Which statement about leaky heart valves is correct?
Tick **one** box.

Leaky heart valves increase blood flow through the heart. ☐

Leaky heart valves stop blood flowing through the heart. ☐

Leaky heart valves allow blood to flow in both directions through the heart. ☐

Leaky heart valves do not affect blood flow through the heart. ☐

[1]

1.2 Apart from being leaky, describe **one** other way that a valve might be faulty.

....

[1]

1.3 Suggest **one** way in which the man's surgeons could treat the leaky valve.

....

....

[1]

[Total 3 marks]

2 A patient is having a heart transplant. (Grade 4-5)

2.1 Why might a patient need a heart transplant?

....

[1]

A donor heart can be transplanted into a patient, or an artificial heart may be used instead.

Donor hearts come from a person who has recently died.
Artificial hearts are machines made from metal or plastic.

2.2 Suggest **one** advantage of using an artificial heart over a donor heart.

....

....

[1]

2.3 Suggest **one** disadvantage of using an artificial heart over a donor heart.

....

....

[1]

[Total 3 marks]

 ☐   ☐   ☐

Topic B2 — Organisation

Health and Disease

1 Diseases can lead to poor health. (Grade 3-4)

1.1 What is health?

....

[1]

1.2 List **two** factors other than disease that can cause poor health.

1. ....

2. ....

[2]

1.3 What is the difference between a communicable disease and a non-communicable disease?
Tick **one** box.

They are caused by different types of pathogens. ☐

Only communicable diseases can spread between people. ☐

Only non-communicable diseases can spread between people. ☐

[1]

[Total 4 marks]

2 AIDS is a disease caused by a virus.
People with AIDS have a weakened immune system. (Grade 4-5)

2.1 Explain why a person with AIDS is likely to get other diseases.

....

....

[2]

2.2 Give **one** other example of how different diseases can interact.

....

....

[1]

2.2 The virus that causes AIDs can be passed between people during sexual intercourse.

Is AIDs a communicable or non-communicable disease?
Give a reason for your answer.

....

....

[1]

[Total 4 marks]

Topic B2 — Organisation

Risk Factors for Non-Communicable Diseases

1 Substances in a person's environment can be risk factors for certain diseases. *(Grade 4-5)*

1.1 What is meant by a risk factor for a disease?

....

....

[1]

1.2 Other than substances in the environment, state **two** types of risk factor.

1. ....

2. ....

[2]

1.3 Obesity is a risk factor for many different diseases.
Name **one** disease that obesity is a risk factor for.

....

[1]

[Total 4 marks]

2 A patient has been diagnosed with cardiovascular disease. *(Grade 4-5)*

2.1 Give **two** risk factors that might have contributed to the patient developing cardiovascular disease.

1. ....

2. ....

[2]

2.2 Suggest **one** reason why non-communicable diseases can be expensive for an individual.

....

....

[1]

2.3 Suggest **one** reason why non-communicable diseases can be expensive for a country.

....

....

[1]

[Total 4 marks]

Exam Practice Tip
Scientists find risk factors by looking for correlations in data. Many risk factors don't directly cause a disease, but they do make it more likely. A person is even more likely to get a disease if they have several risk factors for it.

Cancer

Tumours can be benign or malignant. Draw lines to match the types of tumour on the left with each characteristic on the right that applies to them.

Malignant Tumours

Are cancerous

Are not cancerous

Benign Tumours

Can spread to other parts of the body

1 There are many risk factors for cancer. **Grade 3-4**

1.1 Give **one** example of a **lifestyle factor** which increases the risk of getting cancer.

....

[1]

1.2 Apart from lifestyle factors, give **one** other type of risk factor for cancer.

....

[1]

[Total 2 marks]

2 A tumour is a mass of cells. **Grade 4-5**

2.1 What do tumours result from? Tick **one** box.

| Rapid cell death | ☐ | No cell division | ☐ |
| Slow cell division | ☐ | Uncontrolled cell division | ☐ |

[1]

Figure 1 shows two tumours in a person's body.
The secondary tumour was formed from the original tumour.

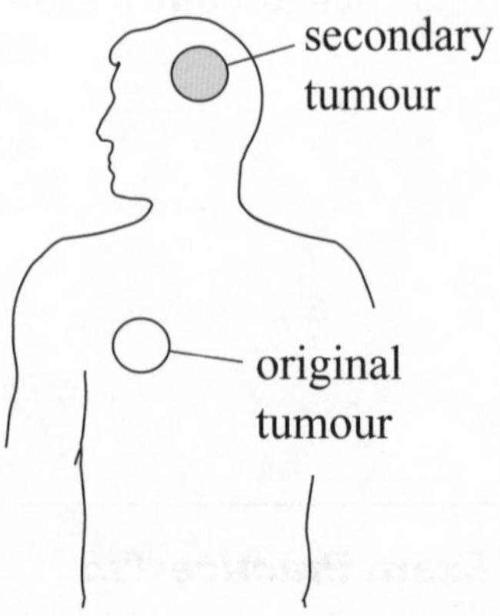

2.2 Explain how secondary tumours form in the body.

Figure 1

secondary tumour

....

....

....

original tumour

....

[2]

[Total 3 marks]

Plant Cell Organisation

1   Leaves have many different types of tissue.   Grade 1-3

1.1   Draw **one** line to match each tissue on the left with its function on the right.

Function

Tissue

epidermal	transports water into the leaf
meristem	covers the upper and lower surface of the leaf
xylem	absorbs water from the soil
	causes growth at the tips of roots and shoots

[3]

1.2   Which of the following answers should be used to complete the sentence?
Write the correct letter, **A**, **B** or **C**, in the box below.

A   organ

B   organ system

C   tissue system

A leaf is an example of a plant ☐ .

[1]

[Total 4 marks]

2   **Figure 1** shows a diagram of a palisade cell.   Grade 4-5

Figure 1

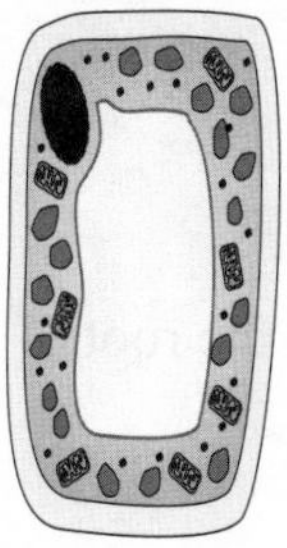

2.1   Explain why most palisade cells are found near the top of a leaf.

....

....

[2]

2.2   Give **one** way in which the structure of a palisade cell helps it to carry out its function.

....

[1]

2.3   Name a tissue inside the leaf that is specialised for gas exchange.

....

[1]

[Total 4 marks]

 ☐   ☐   ☺ ☐

Topic B2 — Organisation

Transpiration and Translocation

The diagrams show a phloem tube and a xylem tube.
In the spaces below, write down which one is the phloem tube and which one is the xylem tube.

elongated cells

end wall with pores

hollow tube

cell wall
strengthened
with lignin

A: ....

B: ....

1   Xylem and phloem transport substances through a plant.   **Grade 1-3**

1.1   What does the xylem transport?
Tick **two** boxes.

mineral ions ☐   protein ☐   sugar ☐   water ☐   starch ☐

[2]

1.2   Which statement about transport in the phloem is correct?
Tick **one** box.

It only occurs in the leaves.   ☐

It is called transpiration.   ☐

It moves sugar around the plant.   ☐

It only moves substances upwards from the roots.   ☐

[1]

[Total 3 marks]

2   Complete the following passage by filling in the blanks.   **Grade 3-4**

Use words from the box. Each word can only be used once.

transpiration	translocation	condensation	evaporation

The process by which water is lost from a plant is called ....

It is caused by the .... and diffusion of water from a plant's surface.

The transport of sugars around the plant is called ....

[Total 3 marks]

Transpiration and Stomata

1   **Figure 1** shows what the surface of a leaf looks like under a microscope.

Figure 1

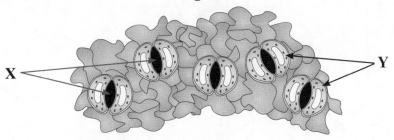

X .... Y

1.1 Name the structures labelled **X** and **Y** in **Figure 1**.

X ....   Y ....

[2]

1.2 What is the function of the structures labelled **Y**?

....

....

[2]

[Total 4 marks]

2   Some students were investigating the effect of air flow on the rate of transpiration.
To do so, they measured the water uptake of a plant in still and moving air.
The rate of water uptake is assumed to be equal to the transpiration rate.

Table 1 shows the students' results.

Table 1

	Repeat	1	2	3	4	5	Mean
Water uptake in 30 minutes (cm³)	Still Air	1.2	1.2	1.0	0.8	1.1	1.1
	Moving Air	2.0	1.8	2.3	1.9	1.7	**X**

2.1 Calculate the value of **X** in **Table 1**.
Give your answer to 2 significant figures.

X = ... cm³

[2]

2.2 Describe the relationship between air flow around the plant and transpiration rate.

....

[1]

2.3 Explain the effect of air flow on the rate of transpiration.

....

....

....

[2]

[Total 5 marks]

Topic B2 — Organisation

Communicable Disease

Circle the word below which is **not** a type of pathogen.

bacteria   insects   protists

viruses   fungi

---

1   What is a pathogen? Tick **one** box.   Grade 1-3

A type of disease. ☐

A microorganism that causes disease. ☐

Something used to prevent the spread of disease. ☐

Something used to treat a disease. ☐

[Total 1 mark]

---

2   There are different ways to prevent or reduce the spread of disease.   Grade 3-4

2.1   Vectors are organisms that spread disease.
Give **one** way that vectors can be stopped from passing on diseases.

....

....

[1]

2.2   Give **one** other way that humans can help prevent the spread of a disease.

....

[1]

[Total 2 marks]

---

3   Oliver has the common cold.
The common cold is a communicable disease.   Grade 4-5

3.1   What is meant by the term 'communicable disease'?

....

[1]

3.2   Oliver uses a tissue when he coughs and sneezes.
Suggest how this helps to prevent others from catching his cold.

....

....

[2]

[Total 3 marks]

Bacterial Diseases

1   *Salmonella* food poisoning in humans is caused by a type of bacterium.   **Grade 4-5**

1.1   Symptoms of *Salmonella* food poisoning include fever and vomiting.
What substances are produced by *Salmonella* bacteria that cause these symptoms?

....

[1]

1.2   Give **two** ways that somebody could get *Salmonella* food poisoning.

1. ....

2. ....

[2]

1.3   In the UK, poultry are vaccinated against *Salmonella*.
Why it is important to vaccinate poultry?

....

....

....

[2]

[Total 5 marks]

2   Gonorrhoea is a disease that can affect both men and women.   **Grade 4-5**

2.1   How is gonorrhoea spread from person to person?

....

[1]

2.2   State **two** symptoms of the disease in women.

1. ....

2. ....

[2]

2.3   Name the antibiotic that was previously used to treat people infected with gonorrhoea.

....

[1]

2.4   Why is the antibiotic in **2.3** no longer able to effectively treat gonorrhoea?

....

[1]

2.5   Name **one** barrier method of contraception that prevents the spread of gonorrhoea.

....

[1]

[Total 6 marks]

Topic B3 — Infection and Response

Viral Diseases

1 Measles is a highly infectious disease. (Grade 1-3)

1.1 What are the symptoms of measles?
Tick **two** boxes.

fever ☐   constipation ☐   yellow discharge ☐   red skin rash ☐   painful urination ☐

[2]

1.2 What can be given to prevent someone from developing measles?
Tick **one** box.

antibiotics ☐   antiretrovirals ☐   a vaccination ☐   aspirin ☐

[1]

[Total 3 marks]

2 The tobacco mosaic virus (TMV) affects many species of plants. (Grade 3-4)

2.1 Name **one** species of plant that can be attacked by the tobacco mosaic virus.

....

[1]

2.2 Which of the following plants, **A**, **B** or **C**, is infected with TMV?

A   yellow leaves

B   leaves lost

C   green leaf   discoloured patches

Your answer = ...

[1]

[Total 2 marks]

3 A virus called HIV causes a disease known as AIDS. (Grade 4-5)

3.1 What type of drug can be used to control HIV?

....

[1]

3.2 What system in the body does HIV attack?

....

[1]

3.3 Describe how viruses such as HIV cause cell damage.

....

....

[2]

[Total 4 marks]

Fungal and Protist Diseases

Fill in the gaps in the passage about malaria. Use words on the left.
Not all of the words will be used.

protist

fungus

fever

vectors

Malaria is caused by a ....

Mosquitoes are the .... that carry the malaria pathogen to humans.

Malaria causes repeating episodes of ....

1   **Figure 1** shows a rose plant affected by a fungal disease.

Figure 1

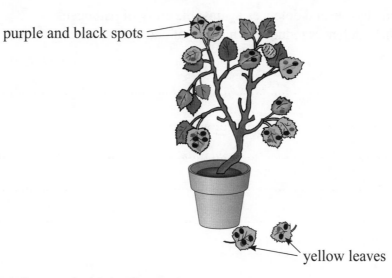

purple and black spots

yellow leaves

1.1 Name the fungal disease shown in **Figure 1**.

....

[1]

A gardener notices that one of her rose plants has the disease shown in **Figure 1**.
She is worried that the rest of her rose plants may also become infected.

1.2 Give **one** way that the disease could spread to other rose plants in her garden.

....

[1]

1.3 Describe how the gardener could treat the disease and stop it from spreading.

....

....

....

[3]

[Total 5 marks]

Topic B3 — Infection and Response

Fighting Disease

1 Different types of white blood cell have different roles in the immune system.

Complete the sentences below. Use words from the box.

| phagocytosis | dissolve | antitoxins | antibodies | digest |

Some white blood cells engulf and .... pathogens.

This is called ....

Other white blood cells produce proteins that lock onto invading pathogens.

These proteins are called ....

[Total 3 marks]

2* The human body has several defences against the entry of pathogens.
Explain how these defences reduce the number of pathogens entering the body.

....

....

....

....

....

....

....

....

....

....

....

....

....

[Total 6 marks]

Exam Practice Tip

Don't panic when you get to a 6 mark question in the exams. Read the question through carefully, then stop and think before you answer. First work out what the question is asking you to write about. Then write down the points you want to make, in an order that makes sense. Make sure you make enough points to get yourself as many marks as possible.

Fighting Disease — Vaccination

1 Children are often vaccinated against measles.

1.1 What is usually injected into the body during a vaccination?
Tick **one** box.

antibiotics ☐

antibodies ☐

dead or inactive pathogens ☐

active pathogens ☐

[1]

1.2 How should a child's white blood cells respond to a vaccination?

....

[1]

[Total 2 marks]

2 Two children become infected with the measles pathogen.
One child has been vaccinated against measles and the other has not.

Figure 1 shows how the concentration of the measles antibody in each child's bloodstream changes after infection with the measles pathogen.

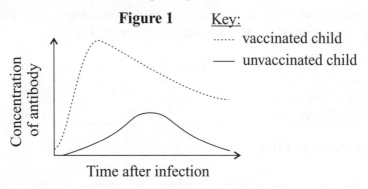

Figure 1   Key:
...... vaccinated child
—— unvaccinated child

Concentration of antibody

Time after infection

Using **Figure 1**, describe how antibody production differs between the vaccinated child and the unvaccinated child.

....

....

....

[Total 2 marks]

Fighting Disease — Drugs

1 A student has a sore throat. Her doctor says it is caused by a virus. **Grade 3-4**

1.1 The student says: "My sore throat cannot be treated with antibiotics."
Is the student correct? Give a reason for your answer.

....

....

[1]

1.2 Name a type of drug that the student could use to reduce her symptoms.

....

[1]

[Total 2 marks]

2 A hospital records the number of cases of infections that are caused by antibiotic-resistant bacteria each year. The figures for three years are shown in **Table 1**. **Grade 4-5**

Table 1

Year	2013	2014	2015
No. of infections	84	102	153

2.1 Describe the trend shown in **Table 1**.

....

[1]

2.2 Suggest why doctors in the hospital might be concerned about the trend shown in **Table 1**.

....

....

[2]

[Total 3 marks]

Developing Drugs

1   New drugs have to undergo pre-clinical and clinical testing before they can be used.   **Grade 4-5**

1.1   Which of the following is preclinical testing carried out on?
Tick **one** box.

healthy human volunteers ☐

cells, tissues and dead animals ☐

patients in a hospital ☐

cells, tissues and live animals ☐

[1]

1.2   During preclinical testing, scientists test a drug to find out whether it works.
Give **two** more things that the drug is tested for during preclinical testing.

1. ....

2. ....

[2]

During clinical testing, patients are split into two groups.
One group is given the drug. Another group is given a placebo.

1.3   What is a placebo?

....

[1]

1.4   Explain why some patients are given the drug and others are given a placebo.

....

....

[2]

1.5   Which of the following answers should be used to complete the sentence?
Write the correct letter, **A**, **B** or **C**, in the box below.

A   only the patients

B   only the doctors

C   both the patients and the doctors

In a double blind trial, ☐ involved in the trial don't know who is receiving the placebo.

[1]

[Total 7 marks]

Exam Practice Tip

There's a lot going on when it comes to drug development. The best way to learn what's going on is to write out each step of the process in order, in as much detail as you can. Keep going over it till it sticks. In the exam, you could be asked a question about the development of a particular drug — then it's just a case of applying what you know.

 ☐   ☐   ☐   **Topic B3 — Infection and Response**

Topic B4 — Bioenergetics

Photosynthesis

1 Plants produce glucose during photosynthesis. The glucose is then used to make other substances, which have their own uses.

1.1 The words on the left are all substances made using glucose.
Draw **one** line from each substance to its use.

Substance made using glucose   **Use**

Substance made using glucose	Use
starch	storage
fats and oils	making proteins
amino acids	making cell walls
cellulose	storage
	making DNA

[4]

1.2 What else is glucose used for in plant cells?

....

[1]

[Total 5 marks]

2 Photosynthesis takes place inside plant cells. **Grade 3-4**

2.1 Name the subcellular structures where photosynthesis takes place.

....

[1]

2.2 Complete the following word equation for photosynthesis.

.... + water → glucose + ...

[2]

2.3 Which of the following statements is correct?
Tick **one** box.

Energy is transferred from the environment during photosynthesis. ☐

Energy is transferred to the environment during photosynthesis. ☐

Energy is made during photosynthesis. ☐

Energy is broken down during photosynthesis. ☐

[1]

[Total 4 marks]

Topic B4 — Bioenergetics

🙁 ☐   🙂 ☐   😊 ☐

The Rate of Photosynthesis

Which of the following things limit the rate of photosynthesis?
Circle the **four** correct answers.

carbon dioxide concentration   amount of soil   amount of glucose

light intensity   temperature   amount of chlorophyll

1   An experiment was done to test the effect of increasing the carbon dioxide concentration on the rate of photosynthesis. The results are shown in **Figure 1**.

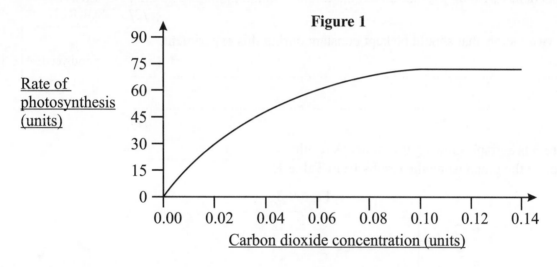

Figure 1

1.1 What conclusion can be drawn from the data in **Figure 1**?
Tick **one** box.

Carbon dioxide becomes a limiting factor at a concentration of 0.10 units. ☐

Carbon dioxide stops being a limiting factor at a concentration of 0.10 units. ☐

Carbon dioxide is a limiting factor at all concentrations. ☐

[1]

1.2 At a carbon dioxide concentration of **0.02 units**, the rate of photosynthesis was **30 units**.
At what carbon dioxide concentration had the rate of photosynthesis **doubled**?
Tick **one** box.

0.00 units ☐   0.04 units ☐   0.06 units ☐   0.08 units ☐

[1]

[Total 2 marks]

Exam Practice Tip

You might need to read a value off a graph in the exam. If so, it helps to get your ruler out. For example: imagine you were asked to read off the rate of photosynthesis on the graph above at a CO_2 concentration of 0.02 units. You'd find 0.02 units on the bottom axis and use a ruler to draw a straight line up from there to the line of the graph. Then you'd draw a straight line across to the rate of photosynthesis axis and read off the value (30 units).

PRACTICAL

2 A student did an experiment to see how the rate of photosynthesis depends on light intensity.
   She measured the volume of oxygen produced by pondweed at different intensities of light.
   Table 1 shows her results. **Figure 2** shows some of her apparatus.

Table 1

Relative light intensity	1	2	3	4	5	6	7	8	9	10
Volume of oxygen produced in 10 minutes (cm³)	8	12	18	25	31	13	42	48	56	61

2.1 State the dependent variable and the independent variable in
     this experiment.

     Dependent variable: ....

     Independent variable: ....
     [2]

Figure 2

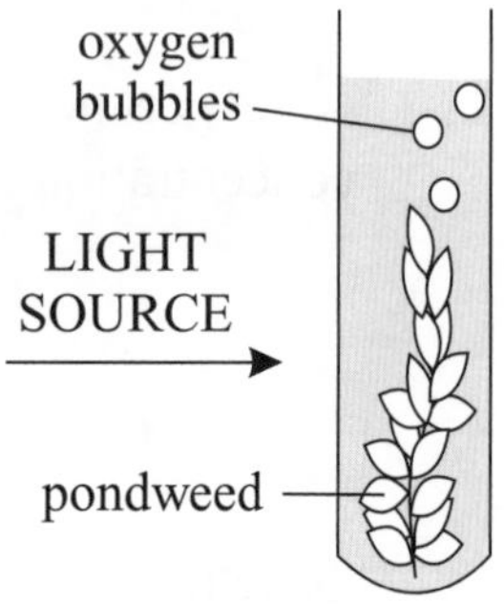

oxygen
bubbles

LIGHT
SOURCE →

pondweed

2.2 State **two** factors that should be kept constant during this experiment.

     1. ....

     2. ....
     [2]

2.3 **Figure 3** is a graph showing the student's results.
     Complete the graph using the results from **Table 1**.

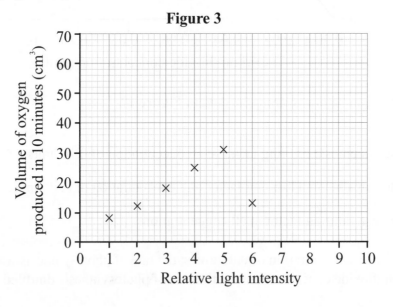

Figure 3

Volume of oxygen produced in 10 minutes (cm³) vs Relative light intensity

[2]

2.4 One of the student's results is anomalous.
     At which relative light intensity is the result anomalous?

     Relative light intensity = ...
     [1]

2.5 Describe what the student's results show about the relationship between light intensity
     and rate of photosynthesis.

     ....
     [1]

     [Total 8 marks]

Respiration and Metabolism

1 Metabolism is the sum of all of the reactions that happen in a cell or the body. Metabolism includes reactions that make molecules.

Grade 1-3

1.1 Complete the sentence below. Use a word from the box.

glycogen	glycerol	amino acids

Lipids are made from fatty acids and ....

[1]

1.2 What type of ion is needed to make amino acids?
Tick **one** box.

magnesium ☐   phosphate ☐   potassium ☐   nitrate ☐

[1]

1.3 Which of these molecules is **not** made during metabolism in animals?
Tick **one** box.

proteins ☐   glycogen ☐   cellulose ☐   lipids ☐

[1]

1.4 Metabolism also involves breaking down molecules.
What is produced when excess protein is broken down?

....

[1]

[Total 4 marks]

2 Respiration is an important chemical reaction.

Grade 3-4

2.1 Complete the following sentences about respiration. Use words from the box.

exothermic	from	endothermic	all	to	some

Respiration is a reaction carried out by .... living organisms.

Respiration is an .... reaction.

It transfers energy .... the environment.

[3]

Figure 1 shows a gull.

Figure 1

2.2 Give **one** example of how a gull uses the energy transferred by respiration.

....

[1]

[Total 4 marks]

Topic B4 — Bioenergetics

Aerobic and Anaerobic Respiration

Draw a line between each substance on the left and its chemical symbol on the right.

glucose

carbon dioxide

water

CO_2

H_2O

$C_6H_{12}O_6$

1   There are two types of respiration, aerobic and anaerobic.

Complete **Table 1** to show which type of respiration each statement refers to.
Tick **one** box in each row.

Table 1

Statement	Aerobic respiration	Anaerobic respiration
It transfers more energy.		
It uses O_2.		
It can produce ethanol and CO_2 as products.		
It is the incomplete breakdown of glucose.		

[Total 3 marks]

2   An experiment was set up using a sealed beaker, with a carbon dioxide monitor attached. The set up is shown in **Figure 1**.

Figure 1

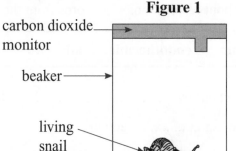

carbon dioxide monitor

beaker

living snail

After two hours, the carbon dioxide concentration in the beaker in **Figure 1** had **increased**.

2.1   Explain why the carbon dioxide concentration in the beaker increased.

....

[1]

2.2   Suggest what happened to the level of **oxygen** in the beaker in **Figure 1** after two hours.
Explain your answer.

....

....

[2]

[Total 3 marks]

Exercise

1 Complete the sentences about exercise below. Use words from the box.

| lactic acid | muscles | brain | glucose | oxygen | ethanol |

During exercise your .... may respire anaerobically.

This causes a build up of ....

It also leads to an .... debt.

[Total 3 marks]

2 A student was investigating the effect of exercise on his own breathing rate. The results are shown in **Table 1**.

Table 1

	Breathing rate (number of breaths per minute)			
	Before exercise	During exercise	One minute after exercise	Five minutes after exercise
Repeat 1	11	16	15	12
Repeat 2	12	15	14	11
Repeat 3	11	15	14	12
Mean	11	15	14	

2.1 Calculate the mean breathing rate five minutes after exercise.

Mean = ... breaths per minute

[1]

2.2 Explain why the student's breathing rate increased during exercise.

....

....

[2]

2.3 Explain why the student's breathing rate remained high one minute after exercise.

....

....

[1]

2.4 Suggest what would have happened to the student's heart rate during the period of exercise.

....

[1]

[Total 5 marks]

Topic B4 — Bioenergetics

Homeostasis

1   Which of the following is **not** part of homeostasis? Tick **one** box.   *(Grade 3-4)*

responding to changes outside the body   ☐

keeping conditions inside the body at the right level   ☐

allowing large changes in conditions inside the body   ☐

responding to changes inside the body   ☐

[Total 1 mark]

2   Human body temperature is kept at about 37 °C.   *(Grade 4-5)*
A homeostatic control system is used to do this.

2.1 Suggest why it's important that body temperature is kept at around 37 °C.

....

[1]

2.2 A man is exercising. As he exercises, his body temperature increases.
The following sentences outline how the man's body temperature will be brought back to normal.
Complete the sentences. Use words from the box.

a coordination centre	a stimulus	effectors	receptors

The increase in body temperature is detected by ....

Information is then sent to ....

The information is processed and a signal is sent to .... ,

which produce a response. The man's body temperature decreases.

[3]

2.3 Shivering is a homeostatic response to a drop in body temperature. It is controlled by the
nervous system. Which other system controls homeostatic responses?

....

[1]

[Total 5 marks]

The Nervous System

1 Information is carried through the nervous system as electrical impulses. Effectors react to these electrical impulses to produce a response.

Grade 3-4

1.1 Which type of neurone carries electrical impulses to effectors?
Tick **one** box.

relay neurone ☐   motor neurone ☐   sensory neurone ☐

[1]

1.2 Muscles and glands are both types of effector. They respond differently to electrical impulses. How do muscles and glands respond to electrical impulses?

Muscles: ....

Glands: ....

[2]

[Total 3 marks]

2 **Figure 1** shows part of the human nervous system.

Grade 4-5

Figure 1

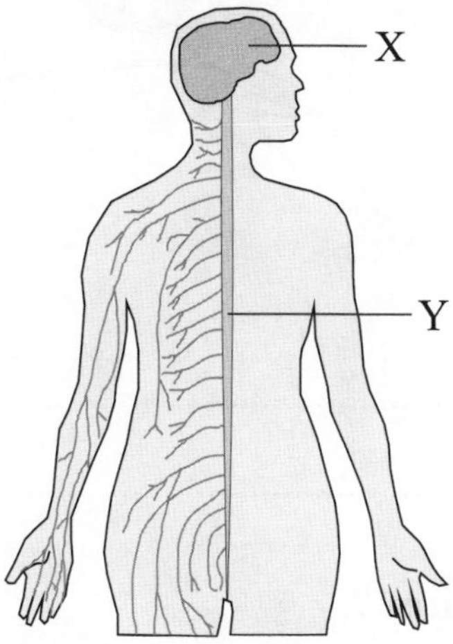

X

Y

2.1 Name the structures labelled **X** and **Y** on **Figure 1**.

X ....

Y ....

[2]

2.2 Which part of the nervous system do structures **X** and **Y** form?

....

[1]

2.3 What is the role of the part of the nervous system formed by structures **X** and **Y**?

....

....

[1]

[Total 4 marks]

 ☐   ☐   ☐

Topic B5 — Homeostasis and Response

Synapses and Reflexes

Which of these actions is a reflex? Circle the correct answer.

Dropping a hot plate.

Running to catch a bus.

Writing a letter.

1 Which of the following sentences is correct? Tick **one** box. *Grade 3-4*

Reflex reactions are slow and under conscious control. ☐

Reflex reactions are slow and automatic. ☐

Reflex reactions are rapid and automatic. ☐

Reflex reactions are rapid and under conscious control. ☐

[Total 1 mark]

2 **Figure 1** shows a reflex arc. *Grade 4-5*

Figure 1

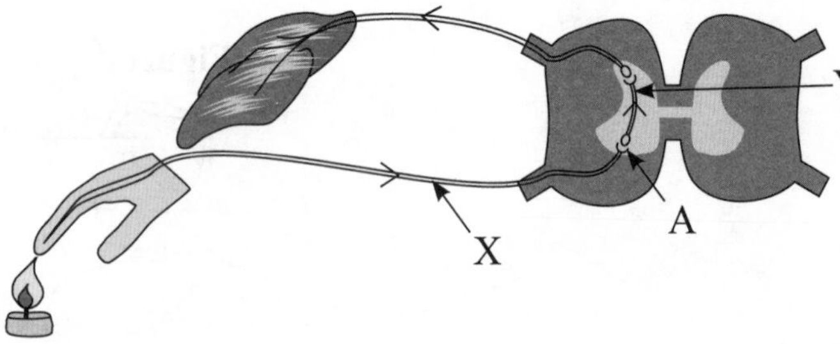

2.1 Name structures **X** and **Y**.

X ....

Y ....

[2]

2.2 What is the **stimulus** shown in **Figure 1**?

....

[1]

2.3 Structure **A** is the junction between two neurones. Name structure **A**.

....

[1]

2.4 Explain how structure **Y** receives a signal about the stimulus.
Your answer should include how the signal is transmitted across structure **A**.

....

....

....

....

[4]

[Total 8 marks]

Topic B5 — Homeostasis and Response

Investigating Reaction Time $\quad$ PRACTICAL

1 A scientist carried out an experiment to investigate the impact of caffeine on reaction time. `Grade 4-5`

- The scientist measured a volunteer's reaction time using a simple test.
- He then gave the volunteer a drink containing caffeine.
- After ten minutes, he measured the volunteer's reaction time again.
- He repeated the test on four different days with the same volunteer.

The results are shown in **Table 1**.

Table 1

	Reaction time (s)				
	Repeat 1	Repeat 2	Repeat 3	Repeat 4	Mean
Before caffeine	0.16	0.15	0.18	0.17	
After caffeine	0.13	0.14	0.16	0.14	0.15

1.1 Calculate the mean reaction time before the volunteer had caffeine.
Give your answer to two significant figures.

Mean = ... s

[2]

1.2 Which statement describes the results of the experiment? Tick **one** box.

Reaction time was slower after caffeine. ☐

Reaction time was faster after caffeine. ☐

Reaction time was no different after caffeine. ☐

[1]

1.3 Each time the scientist repeated the test he got similar results.
What does this say about the scientist's results? Tick **one** box.

The results are repeatable. ☐

There are no errors in the method. ☐

The results prove there's a link between caffeine and reaction time. ☐

[1]

1.4 Give **two** variables that the scientist should have kept the same each time he repeated
the experiment.

1. ....

2. ....

[2]

[Total 6 marks]

Exam Practice Tip

You'll definitely get tested on your practical knowledge in the exams. Make sure you understand what terms such as 'repeatable' and 'variable' mean, so you understand what questions like the one above are asking you. Also, make sure you know the sorts of things that should be kept the same to make an experiment a fair test.

 ☐ ☐ ☐

Topic B5 — Homeostasis and Response

The Endocrine System

1 **Figure 1** shows the positions of some glands in the human body. (Grade 1-3)

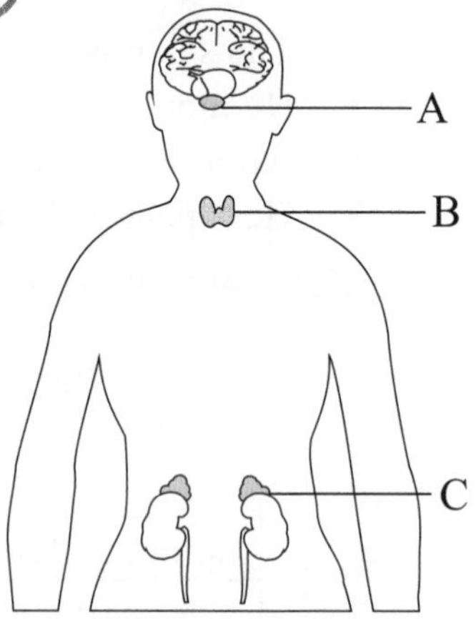

Which part of the diagram, **A**, **B** or **C**, represents the thyroid gland?

Your answer = ...

[Total 1 mark]

Figure 1

A

B

C

2 The endocrine system is a collection of glands in the body that secrete hormones. (Grade 3-4)

2.1 Which of the following statements about glands is correct?
Tick **one** box.

Glands secrete hormones directly into cells. ☐

Glands secrete hormones directly into the blood. ☐

Glands secrete hormones directly into organs. ☐

[1]

2.2 Which of the following statements best describes hormones?
Tick **one** box.

Hormones are cells. ☐   Hormones are chemicals. ☐   Hormones are enzymes. ☐

[1]

2.3 State **two** ways in which the effects of the endocrine system differ from the nervous system.

1. ....

2. ....

[2]

[Total 4 marks]

3 One of the glands in the body is known as the 'master gland'.
This gland secretes several hormones in response to body conditions. (Grade 4-5)

3.1 What is the name of the 'master gland'?

....

[1]

3.2 What is the function of the hormones released by the 'master gland'?

....

....

[2]

[Total 3 marks]

Topic B5 — Homeostasis and Response

Controlling Blood Glucose

1 The concentration of glucose in the blood is controlled by hormones. (Grade 3-4)

1.1 Which gland in the human body monitors and controls blood glucose concentration?
Tick **one** box.

pancreas ☐   pituitary gland ☐   thyroid ☐   testis ☐

[1]

1.2 Which hormone is produced when blood glucose concentration becomes too high?

....

[1]

1.3 Complete the sentences to describe what happens when there is too much glucose in the blood.
Use words from the box.

pancreas	glycogen	insulin	liver

When there is too much glucose in the blood, some of it moves into the ....

The glucose is then changed into .... so it can be stored.

[2]

[Total 4 marks]

2 Diabetes exists in two different forms, Type 1 and Type 2. (Grade 4-5)

2.1 Which of the following statements describes **Type 1** diabetes?
Tick **one** box.

The body produces too little glucose. ☐

The body becomes resistant to its own insulin. ☐

The body produces too much insulin. ☐

The body produces little or no insulin. ☐

[1]

2.2 How is **Type 1** diabetes treated?

....

[1]

2.3 Give **two** treatments that a doctor would recommend for **Type 2** diabetes.

1. ....

2. ....

[2]

2.4 Give a risk factor for **Type 2** diabetes.

....

[1]

[Total 5 marks]

☹ ☐   ☺ ☐   ☺ ☐   Topic B5 — Homeostasis and Response

Puberty and the Menstrual Cycle

1   Males begin producing sex hormones during puberty.   *Grade 1-3*

1.1   What is the main sex hormone in men?   Tick **one** box.

insulin ☐   testosterone ☐   oestrogen ☐   adrenaline ☐

[1]

1.2   Where is the main sex hormone in men produced?   Tick **one** box.

pancreas ☐   pituitary gland ☐   thyroid gland ☐   testes ☐

[1]

1.3   Which of the following is a role of the main sex hormone in men?   Tick **one** box.

stimulating egg production ☐   control of water content in the body ☐

control of blood glucose levels ☐   stimulating sperm production ☐

[1]

[Total 3 marks]

2   Female sex hormones control the menstrual cycle.   *Grade 3-4*

2.1   What is the name of the main female reproductive hormone produced in the ovary?

....

[1]

2.2   What is the name of the process by which eggs are released from the ovary?

....

[1]

2.3   How often is an egg released from an ovary?   Tick **one** box.

Every 7 days. ☐   Every 14 days. ☐   Every 21 days. ☐   Every 28 days. ☐

[1]

2.4   Name the hormone that causes the release of an egg.

....

[1]

[Total 4 marks]

3   During the menstrual cycle, a change in the level of progesterone causes the woman to menstruate (bleed).   *Grade 4-5*

Suggest how the progesterone level changes before a woman starts to bleed.   Explain your answer.

....

....

....

....

[Total 3 marks]

Topic B5 — Homeostasis and Response

Controlling Fertility

All of the methods below are forms of contraception. Circle the **two** hormonal methods.

avoiding sexual intercourse   condom   contraceptive injection   contraceptive patch   diaphragm

1   Some methods of contraception use hormones to control the fertility of a woman.   **Grade 4-5**

1.1   How is an oral contraceptive taken into the body?
Tick **one** box.

As an injection. ☐

As a tablet taken by mouth. ☐

Through the skin from a patch. ☐

[1]

1.2   How do oral contraceptives containing multiple hormones prevent pregnancy?
Tick **one** box.

The hormones stop oestrogen production. ☐

The hormones stop FSH production. ☐

The hormones stop LH production. ☐

[1]

1.3   The contraceptive implant is inserted under the skin of the arm.
Which hormone does it release?

....

[1]

1.4   How does the hormone released by the contraceptive implant prevent pregnancy?

....

[1]

1.5   An oral contraceptive has to be taken daily.
Suggest **one** advantage of the contraceptive implant over an oral contraceptive.
Explain your answer.

....

....

[2]

[Total 6 marks]

Exam Practice Tip

Knowing the roles of the hormones that control the menstrual cycle can be handy when it comes to understanding how these hormones are used in contraceptives. So make sure you've got it all sorted out in your head.

 ☐ ☐ ☐

More on Controlling Fertility

Draw lines to match the barrier method of contraception on the left, to the description of how it's worn on the right.

Method of contraception	Description
diaphragm	worn inside the vagina
male condom	worn over the entrance to the uterus
female condom	worn over the penis

1 There are several different non-hormonal methods of contraception. These include barrier methods of contraception. *(Grade 4-5)*

1.1 How do barrier methods of contraception prevent a woman from becoming pregnant? Tick **one** box.

They break down eggs once they have been fertilised by sperm. ☐

They prevent eggs from being released. ☐

They stop sperm from getting to an egg. ☐

They kill sperm. ☐

[1]

1.2 Name a barrier method of contraception that protects against sexually transmitted infections.

....

[1]

1.3 Some barrier methods need to be used with spermicides.
Explain how spermicides help to prevent pregnancy.

....

....

....

[2]

A couple not wishing to have children do not want to use any form of contraception.
1.4 Suggest how they could avoid pregnancy.

....

....

[1]

[Total 5 marks]

Topic B5 — Homeostasis and Response

DNA

1 DNA makes up the genetic material in animal and plant cells. (Grade 3-4)

1.1 Which of the following statements about DNA is correct?
Tick **one** box.

DNA is found in the cytoplasm of animal and plant cells. ☐

DNA is found in the ribosomes in animal and plant cells. ☐

DNA is found in the nucleus of animal and plant cells. ☐

DNA is found in vacuoles in animal and plant cells. ☐

[1]

1.2 What are chromosomes?
Tick **one** box.

Proteins coded for by DNA. ☐

The structures that contain DNA. ☐

The site of protein synthesis. ☐

The bases that make up DNA. ☐

[1]

[Total 2 marks]

Figure 1

2 **Figure 1** shows part of a DNA molecule. (Grade 4-5)

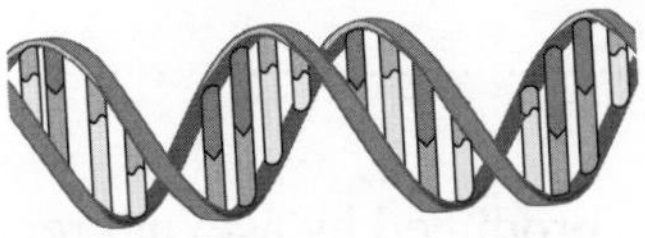

2.1 Describe the overall structure of a DNA molecule.

....

....

[2]

2.2 DNA contains lots of sections called genes. Describe the function of genes.

....

....

[2]

2.3 What is meant by the term genome?

....

....

[1]

2.4 Give **one** reason why it is important for scientists to understand the human genome.

....

....

[1]

[Total 6 marks]

 ☐   ☐   ☐

Reproduction

1   Sexual reproduction involves male and female gametes.

Draw **one** line from each type of gamete on the left to the correct description on the right.

Type of gamete

sperm

egg

pollen

Description

female gamete

male gamete in animals

male gamete in plants

[Total 2 marks]

2   There are different types of cell division in sexual and asexual reproduction.

2.1   Which type of cell division is involved in the production of gametes?

....

[1]

2.2   Name the type of cell division used in asexual reproduction.

....

[1]

2.3   Cells produced by asexual reproduction are called clones.
What does this mean?

....

[1]

[Total 3 marks]

3   There are several differences between asexual and sexual reproduction.

Complete **Table 1** to show if each statement applies to asexual or sexual reproduction.
Tick **one** box in each row.

Table 1

	Asexual reproduction	Sexual reproduction
There is only one parent.		
There is no mixing of genes.		
It results in genetic variation in the offspring.		
There is fusion of gametes.		

[Total 3 marks]

Topic B6 — Inheritance, Variation and Evolution

Meiosis

1 Sexual reproduction in humans involves meiosis. (Grade 4-5)

  1.1 Where in the body does meiosis take place? Tick **one** box.

    all tissues ☐

    growing tissues only ☐

    the skin ☐

    the reproductive organs ☐

[1]

  1.2 Before a cell starts to divide by meiosis, what happens to its DNA?

    ....

[1]

  1.3 How many cell divisions are there during the process of meiosis?

    ....

[1]

  1.4 Briefly describe the results of meiosis.

    ....

    ....

    ....

    ....

[3]

[Total 6 marks]

2 After an egg cell has been fertilised, it divides many times. (Grade 4-5)

  2.1 What type of cell division does the fertilised egg cell undergo?

    ....

[1]

  2.2 The dividing cells form an embryo.
     What happens to the cells in the embryo as it develops in order to form the whole organism?

    ....

    ....

[1]

[Total 2 marks]

Exam Practice Tip

It's easy to get mixed up between meiosis and mitosis. Remember, m̲e̲iosis is the one that makes e̲ggs and sp̲e̲rm. Mi̲tosis makes t̲win (identical) cells. Even if you know the difference, it's still really easy to accidentally write one when you mean the other because the words are so similar, so always check your answer.

Topic B6 — Inheritance, Variation and Evolution

X and Y Chromosomes

1 Chromosomes help to determine the characteristics of individuals, including their sex. (Grade 1-3)

1.1 How many pairs of chromosomes are there in a normal human body cell?
Tick **one** box.

22 ☐   23 ☐   24 ☐   25 ☐

[1]

1.2 How many pairs of chromosomes decide what sex you are?
Tick **one** box.

1 ☐   2 ☐   4 ☐   8 ☐

[1]

[Total 2 marks]

2 **Figure 1** is an incomplete genetic diagram.
It shows how the sex chromosomes are inherited in humans. (Grade 4-5)

Figure 1

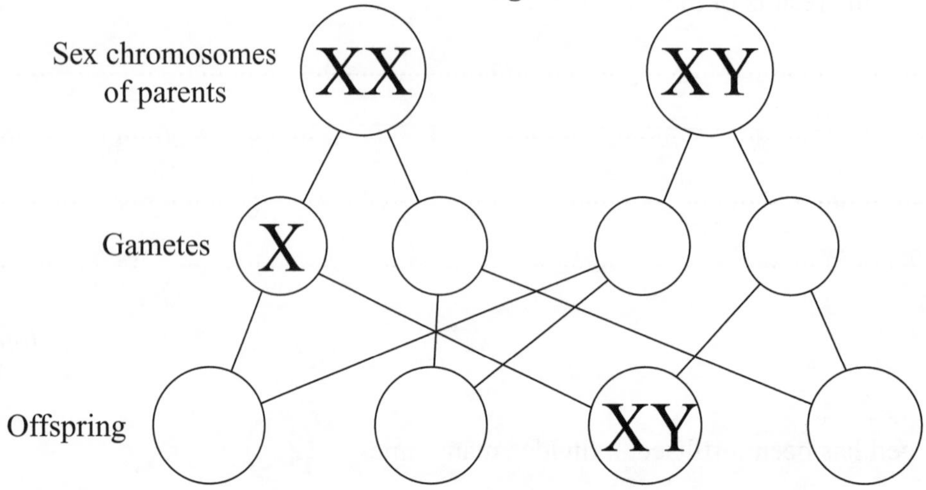

Sex chromosomes of parents: XX   XY

Gametes: X

Offspring: XY

2.1 Circle the male parent in **Figure 1**.

[1]

2.2 Fill in the sex chromosomes of the gametes produced by each parent in **Figure 1**.

[1]

2.3 Complete **Figure 1** to show the combination of sex chromosomes in the offspring.

[1]

2.4 What is the ratio of male to female offspring in the cross in **Figure 1**?

....

[1]

[Total 4 marks]

Exam Practice Tip

Genetic crosses come up quite a bit later on. Most of the time they involve individual genes, but here you're dealing with whole chromosomes. Don't forget that genetic diagrams can be drawn slightly differently too. You may get them in the form of a Punnett square, instead of like the one on this page, so be prepared for both types in the exam.

Topic B6 — Inheritance, Variation and Evolution

Genetic Diagrams

Use the words and phrases to complete the passage below.
You don't have to use every one.

homozygous   alleles   multiple genes   dominant

Genes exist in different versions called ....

If the two versions are the same, the organism is .... for that gene.

Some characteristics are controlled by a single gene, but most are controlled by

....

1   Hair length in dogs is controlled by two alleles. Short hair is caused by the dominant allele, 'H'. Long hair is caused by the recessive allele, 'h'.

Figure 1 shows a genetic diagram of a cross between a short-haired and a long-haired dog. The offspring's genotypes are not shown.

Figure 1

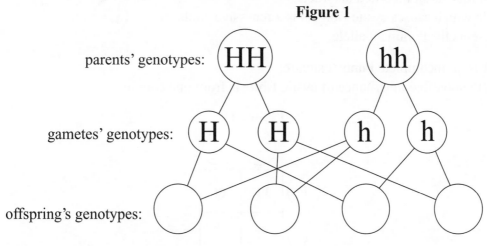

1.1 Circle the long-haired parent in **Figure 1**.

[1]

1.2 All the offspring have the same genotype.
What is the offspring's genotype? Tick **one** box.

Hh ☐   HH ☐   h ☐   hh ☐

[1]

1.3 What phenotype do the offspring have?

....

[1]

[Total 3 marks]

 ☐   ☐   ☐

Inherited Disorders

1 Polydactyly is an inherited disorder. (Grade 1-3)

1.1 What are the symptoms of polydactyly?
Tick **one** box.

missing fingers or toes ☐

faulty cell membranes ☐

extra fingers or toes ☐

[1]

1.2 Which of the following statements about polydactyly is correct?
Tick **one** box.

It is caused by a recessive allele. ☐

It is caused by a dominant allele. ☐

It is only inherited by boys. ☐

Two copies of the allele are needed for an individual to have polydactyly. ☐

[1]

[Total 2 marks]

2 Cystic fibrosis is an inherited disorder.
The allele which causes cystic fibrosis is a recessive allele, 'f'. (Grade 4-5)
'F' represents the dominant allele.

Figure 1 is an incomplete Punnett square.
It shows the possible inheritance of cystic fibrosis from one couple.

Figure 1

	F	F
F	FF	Ff
F	FF	

2.1 Complete the Punnett square to show:
• the missing gametes' genotypes,
• the missing offspring's genotype.

[2]

2.2 What proportion of the possible offspring are heterozygous?

....

[1]

2.3 What proportion of the possible offspring have cystic fibrosis?

....

[1]

[Total 4 marks]

Family Trees and Embryo Screening

1   **Figure 1** shows a family tree.
    The family have a history of an inherited disorder.

Figure 1

Freddy   Zelda

Arthur   Jane   Hilda   Buster

Key
☐ Male   ○ Female

■ ● Have the disorder

◧ ◑ Carrier of the disorder but unaffected

☐ ○ Unaffected and not a carrier

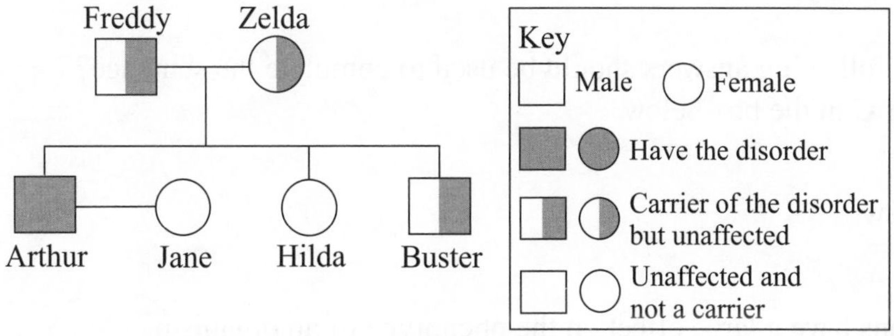

1.1 Which family member is **not** a carrier of the disorder?
    Tick **one** box.

Hilda ☐   Freddy ☐   Zelda ☐   Buster ☐

[1]

The disorder is caused by a recessive allele, 'd'. The dominant allele is 'D'.

1.2 What is **Arthur's** genotype?
    Tick **one** box.

DD ☐   Dd ☐   dd ☐   d ☐

[1]

1.3 What is **Zelda's** genotype?

....

[1]

[Total 3 marks]

2   Embryos can be screened for genetic disorders like cystic fibrosis.
    The results of screening sometimes results in the embryo being destroyed.
    There are lots of arguments for and against embryo screening.

2.1 Give **one** argument **against** embryo screening.

....

....

[1]

2.2 Give **one** argument **for** embryo screening.

....

....

[1]

[Total 2 marks]

Topic B6 — Inheritance, Variation and Evolution

Variation

1 Mutations can lead to variation in an organism. (Grade 1-3)

1.1 What is a mutation?

....

[1]

1.2 Which of the following answers should be used to complete the sentence?
Write **A**, **B** or **C** in the box below.

A   Most

B   Very few

C   All

[ ] mutations have a large effect on the phenotype of an organism.

[1]

[Total 2 marks]

2 **Figure 1** shows two plants of different species, **A** and **B**.
Both plants were grown in the same controlled environmental conditions in a greenhouse. (Grade 3-4)

Figure 1

A   **B**

Give **one** example of a difference between plants **A** and **B** which is likely to be due to
genetic variation.

....

[Total 1 mark]

3 Helen and Stephanie are identical twins. This means they have identical DNA. (Grade 4-5)

Helen weighs 7 kg more than Stephanie.
Explain whether this is due to genes, environmental factors or both.

....

....

[Total 2 marks]

Exam Practice Tip

Remember, variation is usually caused by a mixture of both environmental and genetic factors, not just one or the other.
In the exam, you might get an example of variation that you've never heard of before. Don't worry if you do, all the
information you need to answer the question will be there. Just apply your knowledge.

Topic B6 — Inheritance, Variation and Evolution

Evolution

1   Complete the sentences about evolution below. Use words from the box.

environmental	three	inherited	some	all	six

Evolution is the change in the .... characteristics of a population over time.

According to the theory of evolution by natural selection, ... organisms

evolved from simple life forms that first started to develop over ....

billion years ago.

[Total 3 marks]

2   Over time, many species have become extinct.   (Grade 3-4)

2.1   What does it mean if a species becomes extinct?

....

[1]

2.2   Give **two** factors which might cause a species to become extinct.

1. ....

2. ....

[2]

[Total 3 marks]

3*   **Figure 1** is a photograph of a hare species which lives in a warm climate. It has large ears which help to keep it cool. The size of ears in hares is partly controlled by genes.   (Grade 4-5)

Figure 1

Describe how natural selection could have led to the evolution of hares with large ears, from a population of hares with smaller ears.

....

....

....

....

....

....

....

....

....

[Total 6 marks]

Topic B6 — Inheritance, Variation and Evolution

Antibiotic-Resistant Bacteria

Draw circles to show whether the statements below are **true** or **false**.

Antibiotics are drugs that can kill all pathogens.	True /	False
Bacteria can evolve quickly because they divide very rapidly.	True /	False
Antibiotic-resistant bacteria don't spread easily.	True /	False

1 Bacteria can evolve to become resistant to antibiotics.

Which of the following answers should be used to complete the sentence?
Write **A**, **B** or **C** in the box below.

A normal variation

B natural variation

C natural selection

Bacteria can become resistant to antibiotics by ☐.

[Total 1 mark]

2 *S. aureus* is a bacterium. It can cause serious illness in some people. Some strains of *S. aureus* have developed resistance to the antibiotic meticillin. These strains are known as MRSA.

2.1 **Table 1** shows the different stages that led to *S. aureus* becoming resistant to meticillin. Put the stages in order by writing the correct number (**1**, **2**, **3** or **4**) in the space provided.

Table 1

Number of stage	Stage
....	The gene for meticillin resistance became more common in the population. Eventually most of the population of *S. aureus* had resistance.
....	Individual bacteria with the mutated genes were more likely to survive and reproduce in a host being treated with meticillin.
....	Random mutations in the DNA of *S. aureus* led to it not being killed by meticillin.
....	The gene for meticillin resistance was passed on to lots of offspring. These offspring survived and reproduced.

[2]

2.2 Explain why a person is more likely to become seriously ill if they are infected with MRSA than with a non-resistant strain of *S. aureus*.

....

....

....

[2]

[Total 4 marks]

Topic B6 — Inheritance, Variation and Evolution

More on Antibiotic-Resistant Bacteria

1 How can farmers help to prevent the development of antibiotic-resistant bacteria? Tick **one** box. *(Grade 1-3)*

By regularly treating their livestock with antibiotics to prevent disease. ☐

By restricting the amount of antibiotics they give to their livestock. ☐

By only using antibiotics to treat viral infections in their livestock. ☐

[Total 1 mark]

2 New antibiotics are being developed against resistant strains of bacteria. *(Grade 4-5)*

Give **two** reasons why the development of antibiotics is unlikely to keep up with the rate at which new antibiotic-resistant bacteria appear.

1. ....

2. ....

[Total 2 marks]

3 Antibiotic resistance in bacteria is becoming more common. This is partly due to the overuse of antibiotics in medicine. *(Grade 4-5)*

3.1 Give **one** way in which doctors can help to prevent the overuse of antibiotics.

....

....

[1]

A patient has been prescribed antibiotics by his doctor. He needs to take them for two weeks.

After one week, the patient feels better. He wants to stop taking the antibiotics. His doctor tells him he should complete the course.

3.2 Explain why taking the full course of antibiotics reduces the chance of antibiotic-resistant strains developing.

....

....

....

[2]

[Total 3 marks]

Exam Practice Tip

An exam question on antibiotic-resistant bacteria could ask you to link lots of different ideas together. So, make sure you know the risks of antibiotic-resistant strains to human health, what makes them more common and what we can do to prevent them evolving. There's a lot to remember on this topic, but just go over it a few times and you'll be alright.

Topic B6 — Inheritance, Variation and Evolution

Selective Breeding

1 Selective breeding is used in several different industries. **Grade 3-4**

1.1 What is selective breeding?

....
[1]

1.2 Which of these is another name for the process of selective breeding?
Tick **one** box.

evolution ☐ natural selection ☐ inheritance ☐ artificial selection ☐
[1]

Figure 1 shows four wheat plants (**A-D**). Each plant has different characteristics.

Figure 1

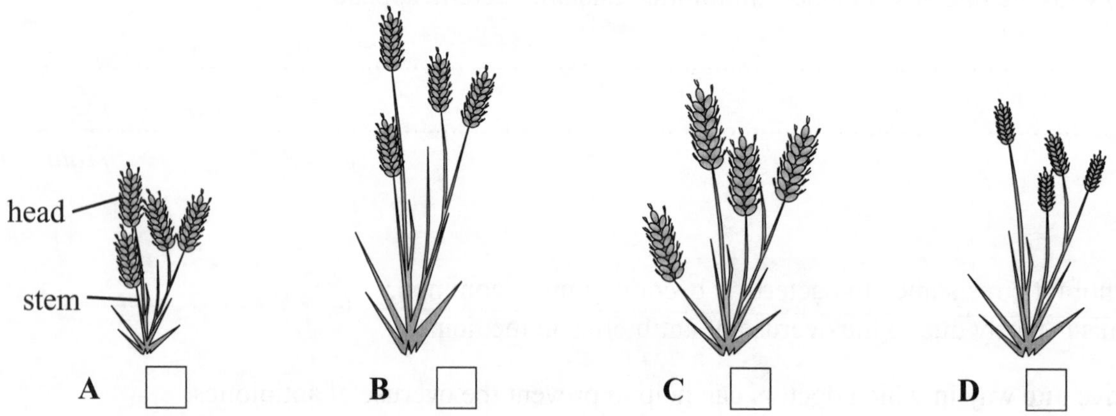

head ——
stem ——

A ☐   **B** ☐   **C** ☐   **D** ☐

1.3 Which two plants should be bred together to get a wheat plant with a tall stem and a large head?
Tick **two** boxes.
[1]

1.4 Suggest why dairy farmers might use selective breeding.

....
[1]
[Total 4 marks]

2 Selectively breeding organisms can lead to inbreeding. **Grade 4-5**

2.1 Inbreeding can make a population more likely to get a disease. Explain why.

....

....
[2]

2.2 Describe **one** other problem which may be caused by inbreeding.

....
[1]
[Total 3 marks]

Topic B6 — Inheritance, Variation and Evolution

Genetic Engineering

1 Genetic engineering has many uses. Grade 1-3

1.1 What is genetic engineering? Tick **one** box.

Choosing organisms with particular characteristics to produce the next generation. ☐

The transfer of a gene from one organism's DNA into another organism's DNA. ☐

Creating the right conditions for the growth of organisms. ☐

[1]

1.2 How can bacteria be genetically engineered to help someone with diabetes? Tick **one** box.

They can be made to produce antibiotics. ☐

They can be made to produce antibodies. ☐

They can be made to produce insulin. ☐

[1]

[Total 2 marks]

2 Crop plants can be genetically engineered to be resistant to herbicides. Grade 3-4

2.1 What is the benefit of genetically engineering crop plants to be resistant to herbicides?
Tick **one** box.

It makes the crop healthier. ☐ It can increase crop yield. ☐

It makes the crop cheaper to grow. ☐ It reduces damage to the crop from pests. ☐

[1]

2.2 Give **two** other ways in which crop plants are genetically engineered.

1. ....

2. ....

[2]

[Total 3 marks]

3 A team of scientists is investigating the number of wildflowers in two meadows.
One meadow is next to a field containing a GM crop. The other meadow is next to a field
containing a non-GM crop. The scientists compare their results for the two meadows. Grade 4-5

3.1 Suggest why the scientists are carrying out this investigation.

....

....

[1]

3.2 Suggest **one** thing the scientists could do to make their results more valid.

....

[1]

[Total 2 marks]

Topic B6 — Inheritance, Variation and Evolution

Fossils

1 Scientists are not sure how life on Earth began. `Grade 3-4`

Which of the following answers should be used to complete the sentence?
Write the correct letter, **A**, **B** or **C**, in the box below.

A there weren't the right conditions for decay

B they were hard-bodied

C they were soft-bodied

Many early forms of life didn't form fossils because ☐ .

[Total 1 mark]

2 **Figure 1** shows a fossilised insect preserved in amber (fossilised tree sap). `Grade 4-5`

Figure 1

2.1 The fossilised insect in **Figure 1** has been protected from moisture and oxygen.
Explain why this has stopped the insect from decaying.

....

....

[2]

2.2 Traces of organisms can also be considered fossils.
Give **two** examples of a trace which may be left behind by an organism.

1. ....

2. ....

[2]

2.3 Apart from preserved organisms or traces left behind by organisms, give **one** other way in which
fossils may be formed.

....

....

[1]

[Total 5 marks]

Topic B6 — Inheritance, Variation and Evolution

Classification

Use the words to complete the Linnaean classification system.
Put the words in the correct order, going from left to right.

species   phylum   order

kingdom, ..., class, ..., family, genus, ...

1   Organisms used to be classified into groups using the Linnaean system.   *(Grade 1-3)*

1.1   Which of the following is the largest group in the Linnaean classification system?
Tick **one** box.

phylum ☐   kingdom ☐   species ☐   genus ☐

[1]

1.2   What does the Linnaean classification system use to classify organisms?
Tick **one** box.

physical characteristics ☐

DNA ☐

the binomial system ☐

[1]

[Total 2 marks]

2   The three-domain classification system was proposed in 1990.   *(Grade 3-4)*

2.1   What is the name of the scientist who proposed the three-domain system?
Tick **one** box.

Charles Darwin ☐

Carl Woese ☐

Niels Bohr ☐

James Watson ☐

[1]

2.2   Which of the domains includes primitive bacteria often found in extreme environments?

....

[1]

2.3   Give **two** groups of organisms which are in the Eukaryota domain.

1. ....

2. ....

[2]

[Total 4 marks]

3 The black-crested coquette is a species of hummingbird. Its scientific name is *Lophornis helenae*.

Grade 4-5

What is the genus of the black-crested coquette?

....

[Total 1 mark]

4 Improvements in our understanding of organisms led to the development of new classification systems, like the three-domain system.

Grade 4-5

Give **two** of these improvements.

1. ....

....

2. ....

....

[Total 2 marks]

5 Evolutionary trees show how scientists think that organisms are related to each other. **Figure 1** shows the evolutionary tree for species **A-K**.

Grade 4-5

Figure 1

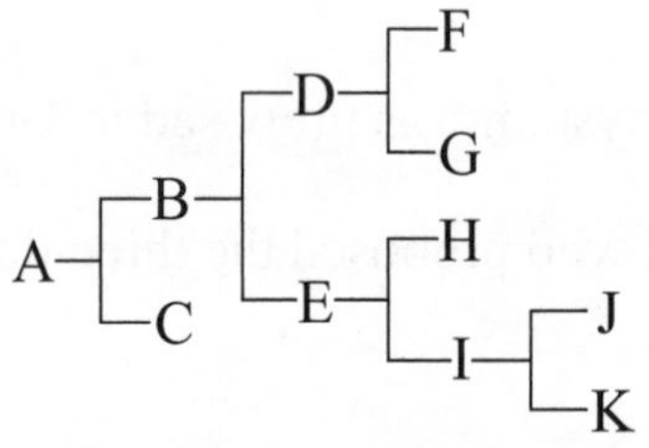

5.1 Give **two** types of data that can be used to make evolutionary trees.

1. ....

2. ....

[2]

5.2 Which species is the most recent common ancestor of species **G** and species **J**?

....

[1]

5.3 Which pair of species, **G** and **H**, or **J** and **K**, are more distantly related?

....

[1]

[Total 4 marks]

Topic B6 — Inheritance, Variation and Evolution

Competition

1 There are different levels of organisation within an ecosystem. *(Grade 1-3)*

1.1 Which of the following levels of organisation contains the smallest number of organisms?
Tick **one** box.

community ☐

population ☐

ecosystem ☐

[1]

1.2 Which of the following answers should be used to complete the sentence?
Write the correct letter, **A**, **B** or **C**, in the box below.

A   one species

B   different species

C   one population

A community is all the organisms of ☐ living in a habitat.

[1]

[Total 2 marks]

2 **Figure 1** shows a woodland food web. *(Grade 3-4)*

Figure 1

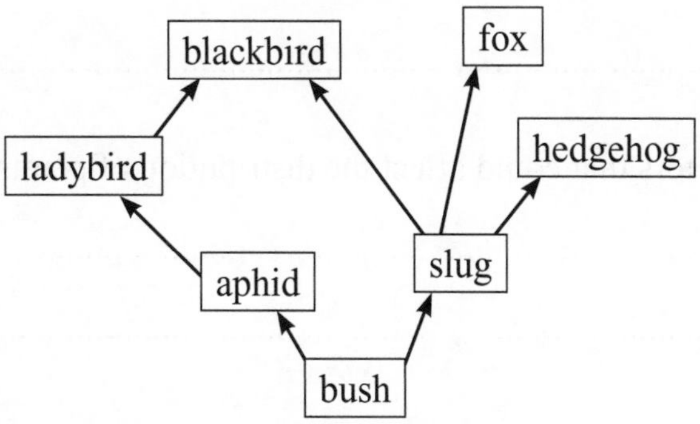

2.1 Which of the following statements is correct?
Tick **one** box.

All the organisms in **Figure 1** are independent. ☐

All the organisms in **Figure 1** are interdependent. ☐

The organisms in **Figure 1** only interact with individuals of the same species. ☐

[1]

2.2 Slugs rely on the bushes for food.
Suggest **one** other factor that slugs may rely on bushes for.

....

[1]

2.3 Apart from food, suggest **two** factors that the **blackbirds** in the ecosystem are likely to compete for.

1. .... 2. ....

[2]

[Total 4 marks]

☹ ☐   🙂 ☐   😊 ☐

Abiotic and Biotic Factors

Biotic factors are the living factors in an environment. Circle **three** biotic factors below.

moisture level   competition   temperature

wind direction   pathogens   predators

1   Abiotic factors can affect the distribution of organisms.   (Grade 3-4)

1.1   Which of the following statements is correct?
Tick **one** box.

Light intensity and temperature are examples of biotic factors.   ☐

Availability of food and carbon dioxide level are examples of abiotic factors.   ☐

Light intensity and carbon dioxide level are examples of abiotic factors.   ☐

Availability of food and light intensity are examples of biotic factors.   ☐

[1]

1.2   Suggest **one** abiotic factor that could affect the distribution of animals living in water.

....

[1]

1.3   Suggest **two** abiotic factors that could affect the distribution of plants growing in soil.

1. ....

2. ....

[2]

[Total 4 marks]

2   A new pathogen is introduced into a population of flowering plants.   (Grade 4-5)

2.1   Describe how the introduction of the new pathogen is likely to affect the plant population.

....

....

[1]

2.2   Bees in the ecosystem rely on the flowering plants for a source of food.
Explain how the introduction of the pathogen is likely to affect the bee population.

....

....

[2]

[Total 3 marks]

Adaptations

1 Some organisms live in environments that are very extreme, such as environments with a high salt concentration.

Grade 3-4

1.1 What name is given to organisms that live in extreme environments?

....
[1]

1.2 Name **one** group of organisms that can live in deep sea vents where temperatures are very high.

....
[1]

1.3 Describe **one** extreme condition, other than a high salt concentration or a high temperature, that some organisms can tolerate.

....
[1]

[Total 3 marks]

2 Camels live in hot, dry desert conditions.
Table 1 shows some of the adaptations of camels to these conditions.

Grade 4-5

Table 1

Adaptation	Reason for adaptation
Long eyelashes	Prevent sand from entering eyes
Very concentrated urine	?
Large surface area to volume ratio	Helps to lose heat
Drinks large quantities of water when available	Helps to replace water lost in hot conditions

2.1 Using **Table 1**, give **one** structural adaptation and **one** behavioural adaptation of the camel.

structural adaptation: ....

behavioural adaptation: ....
[2]

The production of very concentrated urine is a functional adaptation.

2.2 Explain what is meant by a functional adaptation.

....

....
[2]

2.3 Suggest how the production of concentrated urine helps the camel to survive in desert conditions.

....

....
[1]

[Total 5 marks]

Food Chains

On the food chain below, circle the **producer**.

seaweed ⟶ fish ⟶ shark ⟶ whale

1 **Figure 1** shows an example of a woodland food chain. *Grade 3-4*

Figure 1

green plants ⟶ greenflies ⟶ blue tits ⟶ sparrowhawk

1.1 Green plants make their own food. What process do they use to do this?

....

[1]

1.2 What term would be used to describe the greenflies' position in **Figure 1**?
Tick **one** box.

primary consumer ☐

secondary consumer ☐

tertiary consumer ☐

producer ☐

[1]

1.3 Name **one** organism from **Figure 1** which is a predator.

....

[1]

[Total 3 marks]

2 Foxes are predators. Rabbits are their prey. *Grade 4-5*

2.1 The number of foxes in an ecosystem increases.
Suggest what will happen to the number of rabbits in the ecosystem. Explain your answer.

....

....

[2]

2.2 A new disease appears in a rabbit population.
Suggest how this could lead to a decrease in the fox population in the same ecosystem.

....

....

....

[2]

[Total 4 marks]

Using Quadrats

1   A group of students used 1 m² quadrats to compare the population sizes of buttercups in two areas of a field. They collected data from three randomly placed quadrats in each area. Their results are shown in **Table 1**.

Table 1

	Quadrat 1	Quadrat 2	Quadrat 3	Mean
Area 1	15	14	13	14
Area 2	26	23	18	**X**

1.1   Calculate the value of **X** in **Table 1**.
Give your answer to 2 significant figures.

X = ...
[2]

1.2   A student says: "The **median** number of buttercups in **Area 1** is 14."
Is she correct? Explain your answer.

....

....
[1]

The students notice that the buttercups in **Area 1** were growing in the shade.
The buttercups in **Area 2** were growing in full sun.

1.3   Another student says:
"The lower light intensity has affected the growth of the buttercups in **Area 1**."
Do you agree with the student? Give a reason for your answer.

....

....
[1]

1.4   **Area 1** has an area of 1750 m².
Estimate the total number of buttercups in **Area 1**.

.... buttercups
[1]

[Total 5 marks]

Exam Practice Tip

Make sure you take the right numbers from the data when you're carrying out calculations like the ones above — you don't want to lose marks just for writing down a number wrong. And remember, the first significant figure of a number is the first digit that's not zero. The second and third significant figures come straight after (even if they're zeros).

Topic B7 — Ecology

Using Transects

1 **Figure 1** shows a transect line. It is being used to record the distribution of four types of plant in a field.

Figure 1

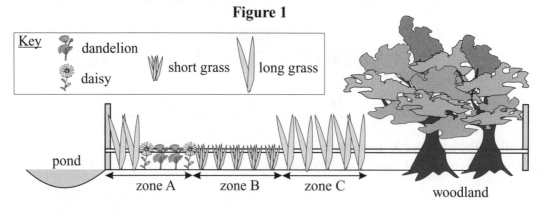

The field is split up into three zones — **A**, **B** and **C**.

1.1 In **Figure 1**, which zones contain only **one** species of plant?

....

[1]

1.2 Dandelions grow best in soils which have a high level of moisture.
Which zone, **A**, **B** or **C**, is most likely to have a high level of moisture?

....

[1]

1.3 Name **one** piece of equipment that may have been used to help collect the information in **Figure 1**.

....

[1]

[Total 3 marks]

2 A student is measuring how much of a habitat is covered by a grass species. **Figure 2** shows the area of a single quadrat covered by the grass. The quadrat is divided into 100 squares.

Figure 2

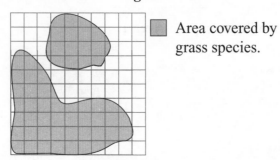

Area covered by grass species.

Estimate the percentage area of the quadrat covered by the grass species in **Figure 2**.

Area covered: .... %

[Total 2 marks]

The Water Cycle

Warm-Up

Find the **three** types of precipitation in the wordsearch below and circle them.

```
g  h  a  v  o  u  p  s  d
r  a  i  n  z  x  q  n  k
f  d  e  g  t  h  y  o  r
s  f  j  h  l  p  e  w  e
p  h  a  i  l  w  e  a  a
```

1   **Figure 1** represents the stages in the water cycle.

Figure 1

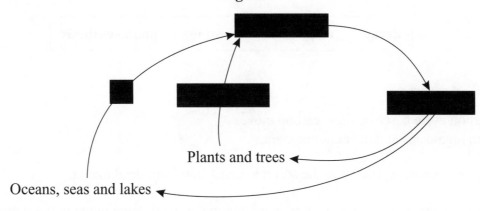

Plants and trees

Oceans, seas and lakes

1.1 Name the process represented by **A** in the diagram.

....

[1]

1.2 What is meant by the term 'precipitation'?

....

[1]

1.3 Explain why precipitation is an important stage in the water cycle.

....

....

[1]

1.4 Suggest how the water in plants can be passed on to animals.

....

[1]

[Total 4 marks]

Topic B7 — Ecology

The Carbon Cycle

1 **Figure 1** shows a simplified version of the carbon cycle.

Figure 1

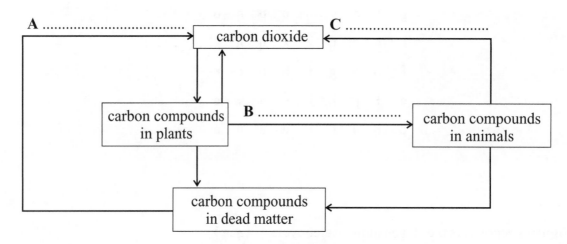

Complete **Figure 1**.
Fill in the labels **A**, **B** and **C** using words from the box.

| decay | respiration | eating | photosynthesis |

[Total 3 marks]

2 The carbon cycle describes how carbon moves between organisms and their environment.

2.1 Explain how microorganisms in the soil release carbon from dead matter.

....

....

[2]

2.2 Describe how carbon from the air can become a part of the carbon compounds in a plant.

....

....

....

....

[3]

[Total 5 marks]

Exam Practice Tip

Make sure you know all of the carbon cycle, not just bits of it. Try sketching out the whole cycle to help you remember it. First write out the different parts, e.g. the air, plants, etc. Then think of the different processes that move carbon around between these parts, e.g. respiration. Draw arrows to show the direction in which these processes move carbon.

Topic B7 — Ecology

Biodiversity and Waste Management

1 Many scientists are interested in the biodiversity of ecosystems.

Complete the sentences below about biodiversity.
Use answers from the box.

species	more	less	habitats	plants

Biodiversity is the variety of different .... in an ecosystem.

An ecosystem with a high biodiversity is .... stable than

an ecosystem with a low biodiversity.

[Total 2 marks]

2 The global population is using an increasing amount of resources.

2.1 State **two** reasons why humans are using more resources.

1. ....

2. ....

[2]

People are also creating more waste and more pollution.
Table 1 shows three different parts of the environment that can become polluted.

Table 1

	Types of pollutant
Air	1. smoke 2. ....
Land	1. pesticides 2. ....
Water	1. .... 2. ....

2.2 Complete **Table 1** to show examples of the different types of
pollutant that can affect air, land and water.

[4]

2.3 Explain how pollution affects biodiversity.

....

....

[2]

[Total 8 marks]

Topic B7 — Ecology

Global Warming

Warm-Up

The sentences below are to do with global warming.
Circle **one** underlined phrase in each sentence, so that the sentence is correct.

Carbon dioxide / Sulfur dioxide is a greenhouse gas.

Oxygen / Methane is also a greenhouse gas.

The levels of these greenhouse gases are decreasing / increasing.

This is cooling down / heating up the Earth.

1   **Figure 1** shows the distribution of a butterfly species in Britain in 1986 and in 2016.

Figure 1

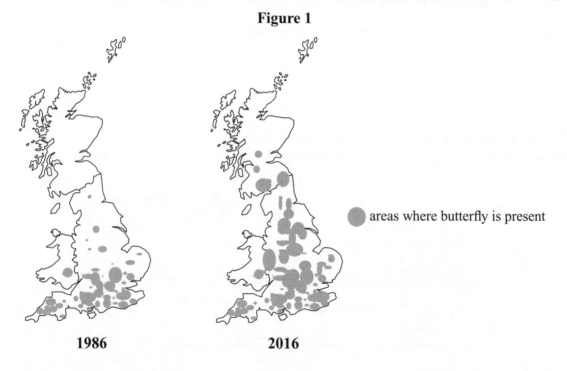

areas where butterfly is present

1986   2016

1.1 Give **two** ways in which the distribution of the butterfly species changed between 1986 and 2016.

1. ....

2. ....

[2]

A scientist thinks that the change in the distribution of the butterfly is due to global warming.

1.2 Suggest **one** other piece of data the scientist might need to find out if she is correct.

....

[1]

[Total 3 marks]

Topic B7 — Ecology

Deforestation and Land Use

1   The destruction of peat bogs can lead to problems.   *Grade 1-3*

1.1   How can peat be used by humans?
Tick **one** box.

as a cleaning product ☐

as an animal feed ☐

as a pesticide ☐

as a compost ☐

[1]

When harvesting peat, peat bogs are drained before the peat is removed.
Because the bogs are drained, any peat left behind will begin to decay.

1.2   What gas is released when peat decays?
Tick **one** box.

carbon monoxide ☐   carbon dioxide ☐   nitrogen ☐   oxygen ☐

[1]

1.3   What problem does the release of the gas you named in **1.2** contribute to?

....

[1]

[Total 3 marks]

2   Human activity reduces the amount of land available for other animals and plants.   *Grade 4-5*

2.1   Give **two** uses of land by humans.

1. ....

2. ....

[2]

Areas of land are often deforested so that they can be used by humans.

2.2   Give **one** reason why an area of land in the tropics may be deforested.

....

....

[1]

2.3   What effect does deforestation have on biodiversity in an area? Give a reason for your answer.

Effect: ....

Reason: ....

....

[2]

[Total 5 marks]

Maintaining Ecosystems and Biodiversity

1 A farmer grows a single type of crop.
As a result, her fields have a low biodiversity.

Grade 3-4

What could the farmer do to increase the biodiversity of her fields?
Tick **two** boxes.

Replace the fences around her fields with hedgerows. ☐

Cut down trees around the edges of her fields. ☐

Increase her use of chemical pesticides. ☐

Allow wild flowers and grasses to grow around the edges of her fields. ☐

Reduce her use of chemical fertilisers. ☐

[Total 2 marks]

2 In some areas, programmes have been put in place to reduce the
negative effects of human activity on ecosystems and biodiversity.

Grade 4-5

2.1 Which of the following could reduce carbon dioxide emissions into the atmosphere?
Tick **one** box.

Setting up more breeding programmes for endangered species. ☐

Using more land for landfill sites. ☐

Increasing the number of power stations. ☐

Reducing deforestation. ☐

[1]

2.2 The government encourages people to recycle as much of their waste as possible.
Suggest how this could help to protect ecosystems.

....

....

[2]

2.3 Breeding programmes are carried out in zoos in many countries.
Suggest how breeding programmes in zoos could increase biodiversity in the wild.

....

....

[2]

[Total 5 marks]

Exam Practice Tip

Humans do a lot to reduce biodiversity (boo, hiss). But remember — there are also lots of ways we can have a positive effect on it. Make sure you're able to describe a few different methods for protecting or increasing biodiversity. You should be able to explain how the different methods work too.

Atoms

Warm-Up

Choose from the words below to fill in the blanks in the passage.

protons   neutrons

electrons   compounds

heavy   light

.... and .... are found in the nucleus of an atom.

.... move around the nucleus in shells.

Compared to electrons, protons and neutrons are ....

1   This question is about the particles inside an atom.   (Grade 1-3)

1.1   Complete **Table 1**.

Table 1

Particle	Relative Charge
Proton	....
....	0
Electron	....

[3]

1.2   What is the overall charge of an atom? Tick **one** box.

Positive ☐   Negative ☐   Neutral ☐

[1]

[Total 4 marks]

2   A potassium atom can be represented by the nuclear symbol $^{39}_{19}K$.   (Grade 4-5)

2.1   What is the mass number of a potassium atom?

....

[1]

2.2   What is the atomic number of a potassium atom?

....

[1]

2.3   How many protons, neutrons and electrons does an atom of potassium have?

protons: ....   neutrons: ....   electrons: ....

[3]

[Total 5 marks]

 ☐   ☐   ☐

Elements

1 Which of the following statements about elements is true? **Grade 3-4**

Tick **one** box.

Atoms of the same element can contain different numbers of protons. ☐

There are about 200 different elements. ☐

Elements contain more than one type of atom. ☐

Atoms are the smallest part of an element that can exist. ☐

[Total 1 mark]

2 Bromine has two stable isotopes, A and B. **Table 1** shows some information about them. **Grade 4-5**

2.1 Complete **Table 1** by calculating the number of neutrons for each isotope of bromine.

Table 1

isotope	mass number	number of protons	number of neutrons	abundance (%)
A	79	35	....	51
B	81	35	....	49

[2]

2.2 Using the information in **Table 1**, state the number of electrons in isotope A.

....

[1]

2.3 Using the information in **Table 1**, calculate the following values:

abundance of isotope A × mass number of isotope A: ....

....

abundance of isotope B × mass number of isotope B: ....

....

[2]

2.4 Calculate the relative atomic mass of bromine. Give your answer to 1 decimal place.
Use the equation:

$$\text{Relative atomic mass} = \frac{\text{sum of (isotope abundance} \times \text{isotope mass number)}}{\text{sum of abundances of all the isotopes}}$$

Relative atomic mass = ...

[2]

[Total 7 marks]

Topic C1 — Atomic Structure and the Periodic Table

Compounds

1   Ammonia is a compound with the formula NH_3. **Grade 4-5**

1.1   Why is ammonia classified as a compound? Tick **one** box.

It contains only one type of atom. ☐

It contains two elements held together by chemical bonds. ☐

It cannot be broken down into elements using chemical methods. ☐

It contains more than one atom. ☐

[1]

1.2   How many atoms are there in a single molecule of ammonia?

....

[1]

[Total 2 marks]

2   The following list shows the chemical formulas of some different substances. **Grade 4-5**

A. O_2 **B.** $NaCl$ **C.** C_2H_4 **D.** H_2 **E.** SO_2Cl_2

2.1   Name substance **B**.

....

[1]

2.2   Identify **two** substances from the list that are compounds.

....

[2]

2.3   How many elements are there in a molecule of substance **A**?

....

[1]

2.4   State how many atoms of each element there are in one molecule of substance **E**.

S: ....

O: ....

Cl: ....

[2]

[Total 6 marks]

Exam Practice Tip

Make sure you know the difference between atoms, elements and compounds — here's a quick round up. Everything is made of atoms (which contain protons, neutrons and electrons). Elements only contain one type of atom (all the atoms have the same number of protons). A compound is made up of atoms of different elements all bonded together. Got it?

Chemical Equations

The word equation for a reaction is shown below:

magnesium + hydrochloric acid → magnesium chloride + hydrogen

For each of the following statements circle whether the statement is **true** or **false**.

1) Hydrogen is a product in the reaction   True   Or   False

2) The equation shows the reaction between chlorine and hydrogen   True   Or   False

3) Hydrochloric acid is a reactant   True   Or   False

4) The equation shows the reaction between magnesium and hydrochloric acid   True   Or   False

---

1   Look at the following word equation: calcium + water → calcium hydroxide + hydrogen   *(Grade 1-3)*

1.1   Name the **two** reactants in this reaction.

....

[1]

1.2   Name the **two** products of this reaction.

....

[1]

[Total 2 marks]

---

2   Sodium (Na) reacts with chlorine gas (Cl_2) to form sodium chloride (NaCl) only.   *(Grade 4-5)*

2.1   Write a word equation for this reaction.

....

[1]

2.2   Which of the following equations correctly represents this reaction?
Tick **one** box.

$Na + Cl → NaCl$ ☐ $Na_2 + 2Cl → 2NaCl$ ☐

$Na_2 + Cl_2 → 2NaCl$ ☐ $2Na + Cl_2 → 2NaCl$ ☐

[1]

2.3   Sodium also reacts with oxygen (O_2) to form sodium oxide (Na_2O).
Balance the equation for this reaction.

$$.............. Na + O_2 → .... Na_2O$$

[2]

[Total 4 marks]

Topic C1 — Atomic Structure and the Periodic Table

Mixtures

1 Which of the following substances is a mixture? **(Grade 3-4)**

Tick **one** box.

copper ☐

calcium chloride ☐

crude oil ☐

ammonia ☐

[Total 1 mark]

2 Mixtures contain different substances. **(Grade 3-4)**

2.1 State the smallest number of substances a mixture must contain.

....
[1]

2.2 Complete the sentence that describes the different parts in a mixture.
Use words from the box.

| change | don't change | electrical | physical | chemical |

The chemical properties of the different parts in a mixture .... when

they're added together. The different parts can be separated from the mixture using

.... methods.

[2]

[Total 3 marks]

3 Air contains many gases. These gases include nitrogen, oxygen and argon. **(Grade 4-5)**

3.1 Is air an element, a compound or a mixture? Give a reason for your answer.

Type of substance: ....

Reason: ....

....
[3]

3.2 Argon can be separated out from air. Will the chemical properties of argon as a separate gas be
different from the properties of argon in air? Explain your answer.

....

....
[2]

[Total 5 marks]

     Topic C1 — Atomic Structure and the Periodic Table

PRACTICAL

Chromatography

1   The first three steps for carrying out paper chromatography of an ink are shown below.   Grade 3-4

    1. Draw a pencil line near the bottom of a sheet of filter paper.
    2. Add a spot of ink to the line.
    3. Pour a small amount of solvent into a beaker.

1.1   Which of the following steps should be done next?
Tick **one** box.

Place a lid on the beaker. ☐

Place the sheet in the solvent so that the solvent is just below the pencil line. ☐

Leave the paper to dry. ☐

Let the solvent seep up the paper until it's almost reached the top. ☐

[1]

1.2   Why is pencil used to make the line on the filter paper?

....

[1]
[Total 2 marks]

2   **Figure 1** shows the result of a paper chromatography experiment to separate the dyes in an ink.   Grade 4-5

Figure 1

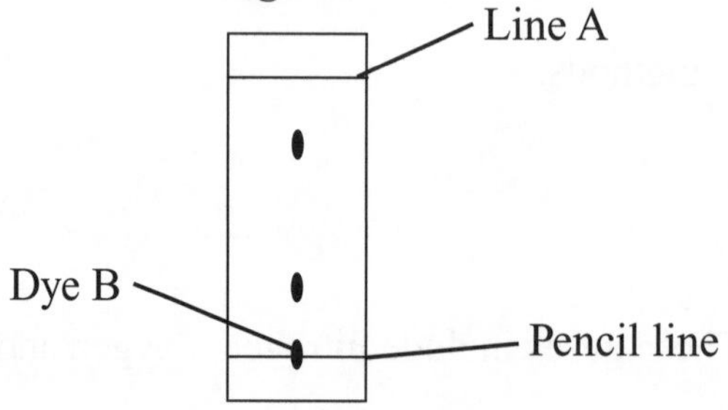

Line A

Dye B

Pencil line

2.1   In **Figure 1** line A represents the point reached by the solvent. What is the name of this point?

....

[1]

2.2   Why does the ink separate into different spots of dye?

....

[1]

2.3   Dye B has stayed on the pencil line.
Predict whether Dye B is soluble or insoluble in the solvent used in the experiment.

....

[1]
[Total 3 marks]

Topic C1 — Atomic Structure and the Periodic Table

More Separation Techniques

1 Filtration is a way of separating substances. **(Grade 1-3)**

1.1 Complete the sentence below that describes filtration.
Use the words from the box.

soluble	insoluble	solids	liquids	solutions

Filtration is used to separate .... solids from ....

[2]

1.2 Which two pieces of equipment would you use in a filtration experiment?
Tick **two** boxes.

Filter paper ☐   Evaporating dish ☐

Bunsen burner ☐   Funnel ☐

[2]

[Total 4 marks]

2 A mixture is made by dissolving substance **A** (a solid) in warm water.
Substance **A** breaks down at high temperatures.
Figure 1 shows the equipment that could be used to separate substance **A** from the solution. **(Grade 4-5)**

Figure 1

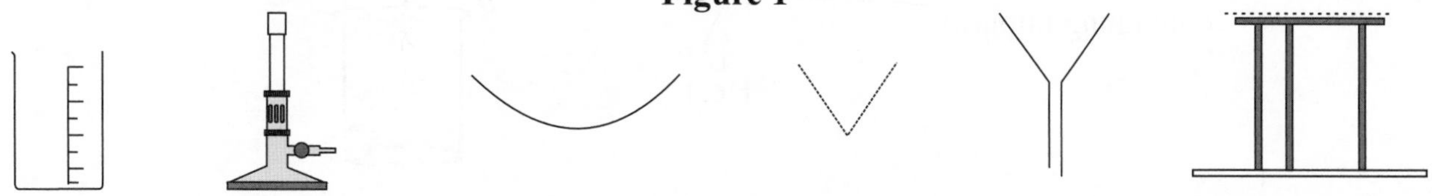

Beaker   Bunsen burner   Evaporating dish   Filter paper   Funnel   Tripod, gauze and heatproof mat

2.1 Name the separation technique that you could carry out using this equipment.

....

[1]

2.2* Write a method that could be used to separate substance **A** from the water using this equipment.

....

....

....

....

....

....

[6]

[Total 7 marks]

 ☐   ☐   ☐   Topic C1 — Atomic Structure and the Periodic Table

Distillation

1 A mixture contains two liquids. The liquids have similar boiling points. (Grade 3-4)

Which of the following techniques would be best for separating the two liquids?
Tick **one** box.

☐ Evaporation ☐ Condensation ☐ Simple distillation ☐ Fractional distillation

[Total 1 mark]

PRACTICAL

2 A sample of butanol, which has a boiling point of 118 °C, was prepared.
The sample contained an impurity with a boiling point of 187 °C. The distillation
apparatus shown in **Figure 1** was set up to separate butanol from the impurity. (Grade 4-5)

Figure 1

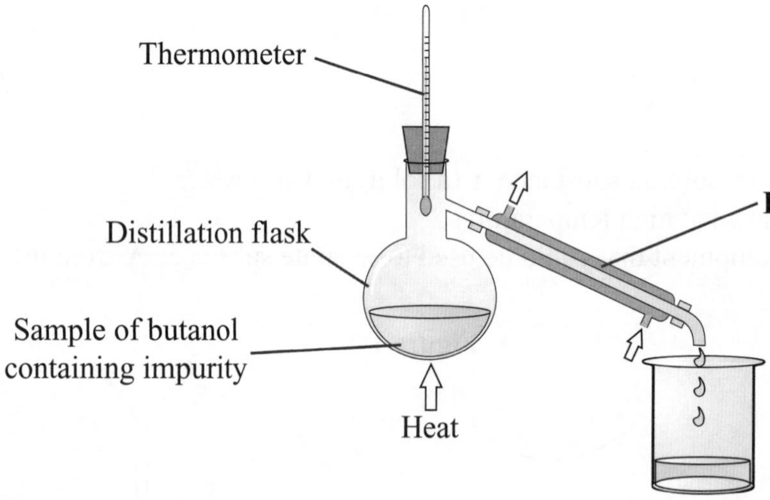

Thermometer

Distillation flask

Sample of butanol containing impurity

Heat

D

2.1 Name the piece of apparatus labelled **D**.

....

[1]

2.2 What happens to the vapour that enters the piece of apparatus labelled **D**?

....

[1]

2.3 Describe how you could use the thermometer to identify when butanol is being distilled from the mixture.

....

[1]

2.4 Suggest why butanol can't be distilled by heating the flask with a water bath.

....

....

[2]

[Total 5 marks]

The History of The Atom

Use the words to label the different parts of the atom shown below.

shell

electron

nucleus

1 Models of the atom have changed over time. (Grade 3-4)

1.1 Which of the following is the best description of what scientists thought an atom was like before the electron was discovered?
Tick **one** box.

Tiny solid spheres ☐   Formless 'clouds' ☐   Flat shapes ☐   Packets of energy ☐

[1]

1.2 Number the models of the atom below in the order they were created. Put a 1 next to the first model created, a 2 next to the second model created and a 3 next to the most recent model.

Nuclear model ☐   Bohr's nuclear model ☐   Plum pudding model ☐

[2]

[Total 3 marks]

2 Scientist's understanding of the atom has changed as different particles have been discovered. (Grade 4-5)

2.1 Draw **one** line from each atomic model to the correct description of that model.

Atomic Model

Plum pudding model

Bohr's nuclear model

Nuclear model

Description

A positively charged 'ball' with negatively charged electrons in it.

A small positively charged nucleus surrounded by a 'cloud' of negative electrons.

Electrons in fixed orbits surrounding a small positively charged nucleus.

Solid spheres with a different sphere for each element.

[3]

2.2 James Chadwick discovered a neutral particle inside the nucleus. Give the name of this particle.

....

[1]

[Total 4 marks]

☹ ☐   ☺ ☐   ☺ ☐   Topic C1 — Atomic Structure and the Periodic Table

Electronic Structure

1   Complete **Table 1** to show how many electrons go in each of the first three electron shells.

Table 1

Electron shell	Number of electrons it can hold
1st	....
2nd	....
3rd	....

[Total 3 marks]

2   Calcium has an atomic number of 20.   (Grade 3-4)

2.1   What is the electron configuration of a calcium atom? Tick **one** box.

☐ 2, 18   ☐ 2, 16, 2   ☐ 2, 8, 8, 2   ☐ 2, 2, 8, 8

[1]

2.2   Calcium has two electrons in the shell closest to the nucleus. Explain why this is.

....

[1]

[Total 2 marks]

3   Electronic structures can be represented in different ways.   (Grade 4-5)

3.1   **Figure 1** shows the electronic structures of an
atom of chlorine (Cl), and an atom of boron (B).
Give the electronic structures of chlorine and boron in number form.

Chlorine: ....

Boron: ....

Figure 1

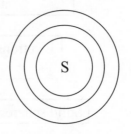

Chlorine   Boron

[2]

3.2   Sulfur has an atomic number of 16.
Complete the diagram to show the electronic structure of sulfur.

S

[2]

[Total 4 marks]

Exam Practice Tip

Electronic structures are a key idea in chemistry, so it's really important that you understand them. Definitely make sure
you know, or can work out (by remembering how many electrons can fit into each electron shell), the electronic structures
for the first 20 elements in the periodic table. Doing this will be really helpful for your exams.

Topic C1 — Atomic Structure and the Periodic Table   ☐   ☐   ☐

Development of The Periodic Table

1 In early periodic tables, scientists ordered elements by their atomic masses.
The modern periodic table is ordered by atomic number. **Grade 3-4**

1.1 Why were early periodic tables ordered by atomic mass and not atomic number?

....

....

[1]

1.2 State **two** problems with early periodic tables.

1. ....

2. ....

[2]

[Total 3 marks]

2 When Mendeleev arranged his periodic table, he left some gaps and also swapped the
order of some elements. This meant the elements weren't ordered strictly by atomic mass. **Grade 4-5**

2.1 Give **one** reason why Mendeleev arranged his table in this way.

....

[1]

2.2 How did the discovery of new elements help to show that
the arrangement of Mendeleev's table was correct?

....

....

[1]

2.3 The discovery of which of the following things also helped to
show that the arrangement of Mendeleev's table was correct?
Tick **one** box.

Neutrons ☐

Isotopes ☐

Atomic mass ☐

Molecules ☐

[1]

[Total 3 marks]

Exam Practice Tip

Mendeleev's table of the elements is a great example of Working Scientifically. Mendeleev came up with an idea, and later discoveries showed that he was right. Make sure you can explain what he did and why it was accepted by scientists.

      Topic C1 — Atomic Structure and the Periodic Table

The Modern Periodic Table

1 **Figure 1** shows the periodic table. $\overset{Grade}{3\text{-}4}$

Figure 1

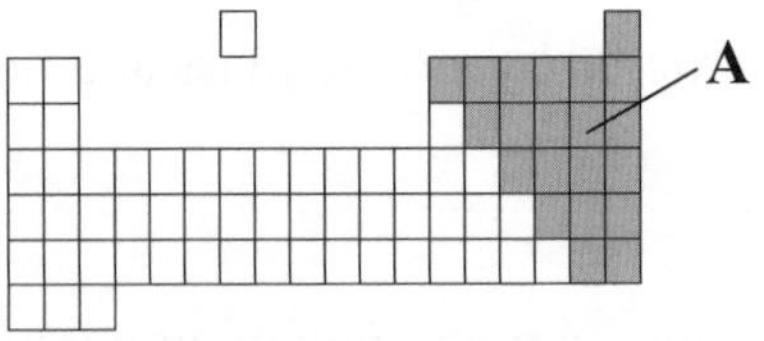

A

1.1 How are the elements ordered in the periodic table?

....
[1]

1.2 What are the vertical columns in the periodic table called?

....
[1]

1.3 What type of elements are found in the shaded area labelled **A**?

....
[1]

[Total 3 marks]

2 **Figure 2** shows the electronic configuration for atoms of three elements, **A**, **X** and **Z**. $\overset{Grade}{4\text{-}5}$

Figure 2

2.1 What group in the periodic table is element **X** in? Give a reason for your answer.

Group: ....

Reason: ....
[2]

2.2 Which period is element **X** in? Give a reason for your answer.

Period: ....

Reason: ....
[2]

2.3 Which **two** elements are in the same period?

....
[1]

2.4 Which element, **A** or **Z**, will react in a similar way to element **X**? Give a reason for your answer.

Element: ....

Reason: ....
[2]

[Total 7 marks]

Topic C1 — Atomic Structure and the Periodic Table

Metals and Non-Metals

1 About 80% of all the elements in the periodic table are metals. **Grade 3-4**

1.1 Describe where metals can be found in the periodic table.

....

[1]

1.2 Which **two** of the following properties are typical properties of metals?
Tick **two** boxes.

Conductors of electricity ☐

Liquids at room temperature ☐

Can be bent or hammered into different shapes ☐

Low density ☐

[1]

[Total 2 marks]

2 Some metals will react with particular non-metals to form compounds made of ions. **Grade 4-5**

2.1 Two elements, with the chemical symbols A and X, react together to form a compound
made of A^{2+} ions and X^{2-} ions. One of the elements is a metal and one is a non-metal.
State which element is the metal and which is the non-metal.

A^{2+} .... X^{2-} ....

[1]

2.2 Fill in the gaps to complete the passage about how metals react. Use the words in the box.

| gain | lose | share | half-full | full |

When metals react, they .... electrons.

When this happens they end up with a .... outer shell of electrons.

[2]

2.3 State **three** physical properties that non-metals are likely to have.

1. ....

2. ....

3. ....

[3]

[Total 6 marks]

Topic C1 — Atomic Structure and the Periodic Table

Group 1 Elements

1 Lithium can react with chlorine. **(Grade 3-4)**

1.1 What is the charge on the lithium ions that form in this reaction?

....

[1]

1.2 What type of compound is the product of this reaction?

....

[1]

[Total 2 marks]

2 The Group 1 elements show trends in their properties. **(Grade 3-4)**

2.1 The density of the Group 1 elements **increases** down the group. Put the elements lithium (Li), sodium (Na) and potassium (K) in order from least dense to most dense.

.... Least dense

....

.... Most dense

[1]

2.2 Draw **one** line from each property to show how it changes as you go down Group 1.

Property	**Trend down Group 1**
Melting point	Increases
Boiling point	Decreases
	Doesn't change

[2]

[Total 3 marks]

3 This question is about the reactions of Group 1 elements with water. **(Grade 4-5)**

3.1 Complete the word equation for the reaction of sodium with water:

sodium + water → .... + ...

[2]

3.2 Potassium reacts more strongly than sodium with water. Explain why.

....

....

....

....

[3]

[Total 5 marks]

Topic C1 — Atomic Structure and the Periodic Table

Group 7 Elements

1 Complete the passage about the Group 7 elements. Use the words in the box. *Grade 1-3*

| one | +1 | seven | halogens | halides | −1 | eight |

The Group 7 elements all have .... electrons in their outer shell.

They can react to form ions with a .... charge.

These ions are called ....

[Total 3 marks]

2 The elements in Group 7 of the periodic table are known as the halogens. *Grade 3-4*

2.1 Which of the following statements about the halogens is true? Tick **one** box.

They are non-metals that exist as single atoms. ☐

They are metals that exist as single atoms. ☐

They are non-metals that exist as molecules of two atoms. ☐

They are metals that exist as molecules of two atoms. ☐

[1]

2.2 Which halogen has the lowest boiling point?

....

[1]

[Total 2 marks]

3 This question is about the reactivity of the halogens. *Grade 4-5*

3.1 Compare the chemical reactivity of chlorine and bromine. Explain your answer.

....

....

....

[3]

3.2 Halogens can react with other elements to form molecular compounds. Of the following elements, suggest which one might form a molecular compound with a halogen. Tick **one** box.

Na ☐   K ☐   H ☐   Cu ☐

[1]

Give a reason for your answer.

....

[1]

[Total 5 marks]

           Topic C1 — Atomic Structure and the Periodic Table

Group 0 Elements

1 The Group 0 elements have similar properties. **Grade 3-4**

1.1 Describe the state of the Group 0 elements at room temperature.

....

[1]

1.2 Which of the following best describes the structure of the Group 0 elements?
Tick **one** box.

molecules containing two atoms ☐

single atoms ☐

ions ☐

metallic ☐

[1]

1.3 The Group 0 elements are unreactive. Explain why.

....

[1]

[Total 3 marks]

2 The noble gases can be found in Group 0 of the periodic table. **Grade 4-5**

2.1 Using the information in **Table 1**, complete the table by predicting the boiling point of radon (Rn).

Table 1

Element	Boiling Point / °C
Ar	−186
Kr	−152
Xe	−108
Rn	....

[1]

2.2 Explain the trend in boiling points as you go down Group 0.

....

....

....

[3]

[Total 4 marks]

> ***Exam Practice Tip***
> You need to know why elements in Groups 1 and 7 are reactive and know what they react with. You also need to know why Group 0 elements don't react. Remember it's all about the number of electrons in the outer shell of the elements.

Topic C1 — Atomic Structure and the Periodic Table

Formation of Ions

1   This question is about ions.   (Grade 1-3)

   1.1   Complete the sentence below.
       Use a word from the box.

atoms	electrons	charges

      Ions are formed when .... gain or lose electrons.

[1]

   1.2   An ion has a charge of +1.
       How many electrons were lost in the formation of this ion?

      ....

[1]

[Total 2 marks]

2   This question is about ions and their formation.   (Grade 4-5)

   2.1   Which statement about the atoms of metallic elements is correct?
       Tick **one** box.

      Metal atoms usually lose electrons to become negative ions.   ☐

      Metal atoms usually gain electrons to become negative ions.   ☐

      Metal atoms usually gain electrons to become positive ions.   ☐

      Metal atoms usually lose electrons to become positive ions.   ☐

[1]

   2.2   There are four different ions shown below. Each one is of a different element.
       Draw **one** line between each ion and its description.

Ion	Description
A^+	A non-metal from Group 6
D^-	A metal from Group 2
X^{2+}	A metal from Group 1
Z^{2-}	A non-metal from Group 7

[2]

[Total 3 marks]

Ionic Bonding

1 This question is about ionic bonding.

1.1 Ionic bonding involves metal and non-metal atoms bonding together.
Complete the sentences. Use words from the box.

negatively	opposite	similar	neutrally	positively

Metal atoms lose electrons to form .... charged ions.

The non-metal atoms gain electrons and form .... charged ions.

These ions have .... charges so they are attracted to each other.

[3]

1.2 Magnesium and oxygen bond together to form the ionic compound magnesium oxide (MgO).
To form MgO a magnesium atom **loses** two electrons and an oxygen atom **gains** two electrons.

State the formulas of the magnesium and oxygen ions in MgO.

Magnesium ion ....

Oxygen ion ....

[2]

[Total 5 marks]

2 The dot and cross diagram below shows the formation of lithium fluoride from its elements.

2.1 Complete the diagram by:
- adding an **arrow** to show the transfer of electron(s)
- adding the charges of the ions
- completing the outer shell electronic structure of the fluoride ion

[3]

2.2 Name the force that holds the ions together in an ionic bond.

....

[1]

2.3 State how you can tell from a dot and cross diagram that the particles
in a compound are held together by ionic bonds.

....

[1]

[Total 5 marks]

Exam Practice Tip

Understanding how ionic compounds are formed can be a bit tricky. Just remember that no electrons disappear, they just move. Make sure you practise drawing some compounds with arrows to show how the electrons move and form the ions.

Ionic Compounds

Circle the correct words or phrases in the passage below.

In an ionic compound, the particles are held together by <u>weak</u>/<u>strong</u> forces of
attraction. These forces are called ionic bonds and act <u>in all directions</u>/<u>in one direction</u>.

1   Potassium bromide is an ionic compound made of potassium ions and bromide ions.

1.1 Complete the diagram below to show the position of the ions in potassium bromide.
     Write a symbol in each circle to show whether it is a potassium ion (K^+) or a bromide ion (Br^-).

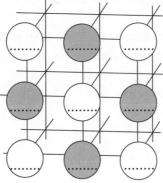

[1]

1.2 Give **one** disadvantage of using the type of diagram above
     to show the structure of an ionic compound.

     ....

     ....

[1]

[Total 2 marks]

2   This question is about ionic compounds.   (Grade 4-5)

2.1 Which of the following properties is **not** typical for an ionic compound?
     Tick **one** box.

     ☐ high melting points   ☐ high boiling points

     ☐ conduct electricity in the liquid state   ☐ conduct electricity in the solid state

[1]

2.2 Name the type of structure that ionic compounds have.

     ....

[1]

[Total 2 marks]

      Topic C2 — Bonding, Structure and Properties of Matter

Covalent Bonding

1 This question is about covalent bonding.

Complete the sentences. Use words from the box.

metal	share	non-metal	covalent	electrons	swap

Covalent bonds form between two .... atoms. These bonds form

because the atoms .... a pair of ....

[Total 3 marks]

2 The diagrams below show dot and cross diagrams of some covalent molecules.

2.1 Draw out the displayed formulas of these molecules using straight lines to represent
covalent bonds. The displayed formula of molecule **A** has been done as an example.

Dot and cross diagram   **Displayed formula**

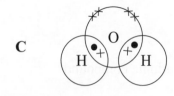

A   Cl — Cl

B

C

[2]

2.2 Write out the molecular formula for molecules **A**, **B** and **C**.

Molecule **A** ....

Molecule **B** ....

Molecule **C** ....

[3]

[Total 5 marks]

Topic C2 — Bonding, Structure and Properties of Matter

Simple Molecular Substances

1 **Figure 1** shows dot and cross diagrams of hydrogen and oxygen atoms.

Figure 1

1.1 Complete the diagram below to show the shared electrons in a molecule of hydrogen (H_2).

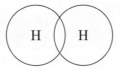

[1]

1.2 Complete the diagram below to show the shared electrons in a molecule of oxygen (O_2).

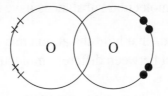

[1]

[Total 2 marks]

2 This question is about simple molecular substances. **Grade 3-4**

2.1 Which of the molecules in **Table 1** is a simple molecular substance?

Table 1

Molecule	Molecular formula	Type of bonding
A	HCl	covalent
B	NaCl	ionic

Write your answer in the box. ☐

[1]

2.2 Explain your answer to question 2.1.

....

....

[1]

[Total 2 marks]

Topic C2 — Bonding, Structure and Properties of Matter

3 Methane (CH_4) is a simple molecular compound.

3.1 Draw a dot and cross diagram to show a molecule of methane.
You should only show the outer shells of electrons.

[2]

3.2 Give **one** disadvantage of this type of diagram.

....

[1]

[Total 3 marks]

4 The bonds and forces in simple molecular substances have different strengths.

4.1 Compare the strength of the bonds that hold the atoms in a molecule
together with the forces that exist between different molecules.

....

....

[2]

4.2 When a simple molecular substance melts, is it the bonds between atoms
or the forces between molecules that are broken?

....

[1]

4.3 **Figure 2** shows two different simple molecular substances.

Figure 2

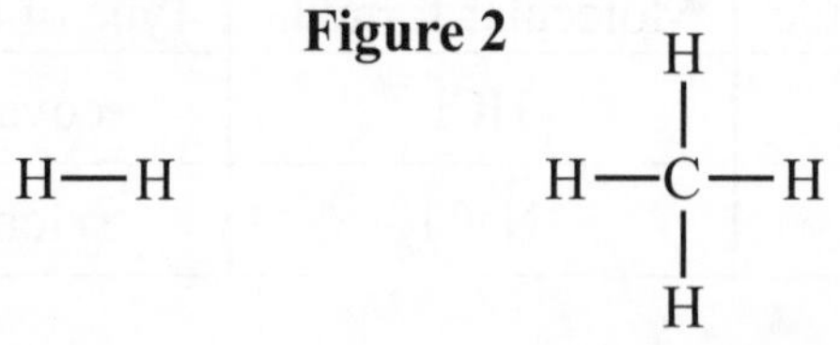

$$H—H$$

hydrogen

$$H—\overset{\displaystyle H}{\underset{\displaystyle H}{C}}—H$$

methane

Methane has a higher boiling point than hydrogen. Explain why.

....

....

....

[3]

[Total 6 marks]

Exam Practice Tip

It's a good idea to learn some examples of simple molecular substances — it'll help you remember what they are.
Keep in mind that they're small and have covalent bonds between atoms. Don't forget to learn their properties too.

Polymers and Giant Covalent Structures

1 Substances that contain covalent bonds can have very different structures.

 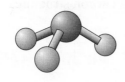 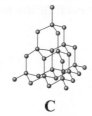 

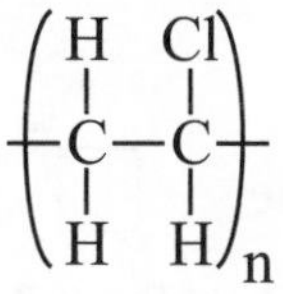

    A   **B**   **C**   **D**

Which diagram, **A**, **B**, **C** or **D**, represents a giant covalent structure? ....

[Total 1 mark]

2 This question is about giant covalent structures.

2.1 Which of the following compounds is **not** an example of a giant covalent structure?
Tick **one** box.

☐ Ammonia   ☐ Diamond   ☐ Graphite   ☐ Silicon dioxide

[1]

2.2 Explain why most giant covalent compounds do not conduct electricity.

[1]

[Total 2 marks]

3 **Figure 1** represents a polymer.

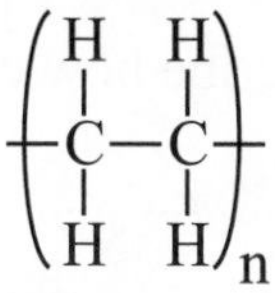

3.1 What is the molecular formula of this polymer?

Figure 1

[1]

3.2 State what type of bonds hold the atoms in the polymer together.

[1]

3.3 Explain why most polymers are solid at room temperature.

....

[1]

[Total 3 marks]

       Topic C2 — Bonding, Structure and Properties of Matter

Structures of Carbon

1 Several different carbon structures are shown in **Figure 1**.

Look at the structures labelled **A**, **B**, **C**.

Figure 1

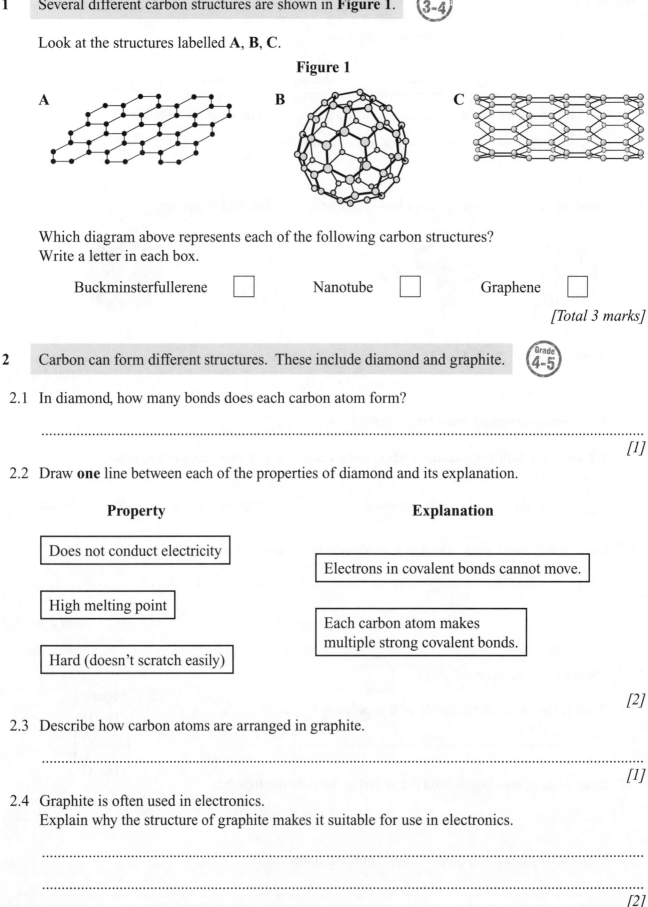

Which diagram above represents each of the following carbon structures?
Write a letter in each box.

Buckminsterfullerene ☐   Nanotube ☐   Graphene ☐

[Total 3 marks]

2 Carbon can form different structures. These include diamond and graphite. **Grade 4-5**

2.1 In diamond, how many bonds does each carbon atom form?

....

[1]

2.2 Draw **one** line between each of the properties of diamond and its explanation.

Property   **Explanation**

| Does not conduct electricity |

| Electrons in covalent bonds cannot move. |

| High melting point |

| Each carbon atom makes multiple strong covalent bonds. |

| Hard (doesn't scratch easily) |

[2]

2.3 Describe how carbon atoms are arranged in graphite.

....

[1]

2.4 Graphite is often used in electronics.
Explain why the structure of graphite makes it suitable for use in electronics.

....

....

[2]

[Total 6 marks]

Metallic Bonding

Circle the elements shown below that are metals.

Copper   **Nitrogen**   **Chlorine**   **Tin**   **Oxygen**   **Magnesium**   **Aluminium**

1   **Figure 1** shows two different metals.   *Grade 1-3*

Figure 1

Which metal shown in **Figure 1** is an alloy?
Give a reason for your answer.

Metal ....

Reason ....

Metal X   Metal Y

....

[Total 2 marks]

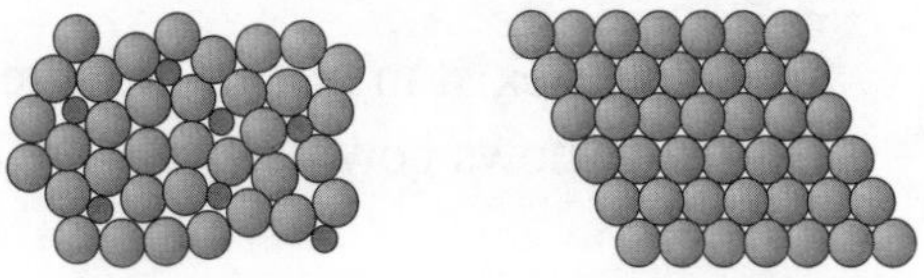

2   **Figure 2** shows the structure of a pure metal.   *Grade 4-5*

Figure 2

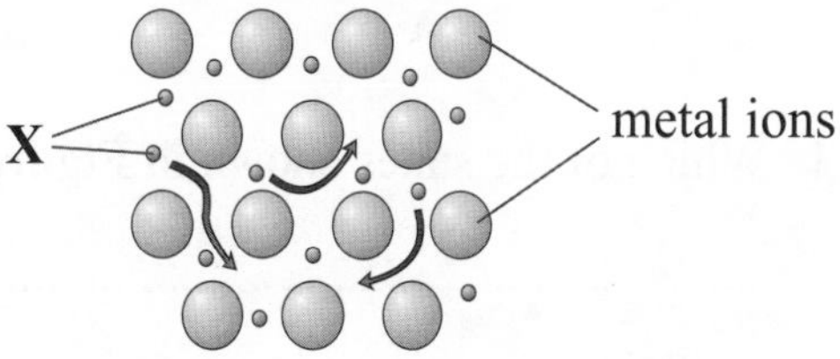

2.1   In **Figure 2** some particles are labelled with an **X**.
Name these particles.

X ⟶   ⟵ metal ions

....

[1]

2.2   Metal atoms form ions that are positively charged.
Explain how they are held together in the structure seen in **Figure 2**.

....

....

[2]

2.3   Metals have high melting and boiling points. Explain why.

....

....

[2]

2.4   A scientist has samples of two different metals, **A** and **B**.
Metal A is pure iron. Metal B contains iron and other elements.
Which metal would you expect to be **easier** to bend? Explain your answer.

....

....

....

[3]

[Total 8 marks]

States of Matter

1 Look at the substances **A**, **B** and **C**, below. (Grade 1-3)

     A: $NaCl_{(s)}$ **B**: $O_{2(g)}$ **C**: $Hg_{(l)}$

1.1 Which substance is a solid? ☐

1.2 Which substance is a liquid? ☐

1.3 Which substance is a gas? ☐

[Total 3 marks]

2 Substances exist in one of the three states of matter. These are solids, liquids and gases. **Figure 1** shows how particles are arranged in each of the three states. (Grade 1-3)

Figure 1

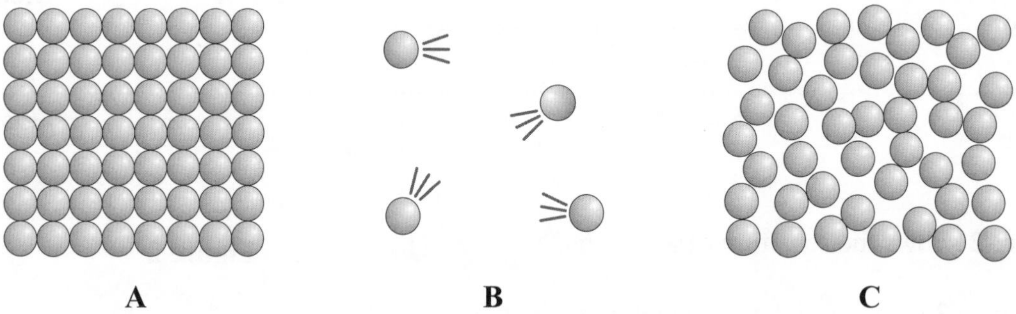

       A   **B**   **C**

2.1 Which of the states shown in **Figure 1** represents a liquid? Give your answer as A, B or C.

....

[1]

2.2 In **Figure 1**, what does each ball represent?

....

[1]

[Total 2 marks]

3 The three states of matter are solids, liquids and gases. (Grade 4-5)

3.1 Place solids, liquids and gases in order of the strength of attraction between their particles.

Strongest attraction   ....

          ↑   ....

         ↓

Weakest attraction   ....

[1]

3.2 When gases and liquids are placed inside a container they change shape. Why does this **not** happen when a solid is put inside a container?

....

....

[1]

[Total 2 marks]

Topic C2 — Bonding, Structure and Properties of Matter

Changing State

1   This question is about changing state.   (Grade 1-3)

In **Figure 1** the arrows represent processes that cause a change in state to happen.

Figure 1

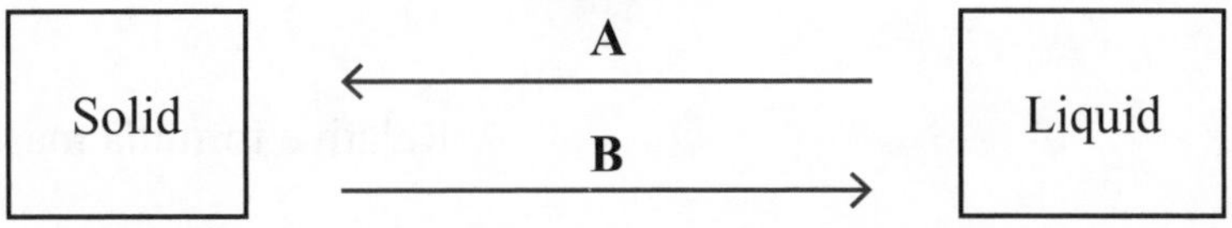

Solid	⟵ A	Liquid
	B ⟶	

1.1   Process **A** causes a liquid to turn into a solid. Name this process.

....

[1]

1.2   Process **B** causes a solid to turn into a liquid. Name this process.

....

[1]

[Total 2 marks]

2   This question is about the processes by which a material changes state.   (Grade 4-5)

2.1   What is the name of the process when a liquid turns into a gas?

....

[1]

2.2   Liquid X turns into a gas at a very high temperature.
What does this suggest about the strength of the bonds between the particles in liquid X?

....

[1]

[Total 2 marks]

3   Use the data in **Table 1** to help you answer the questions that follow: (Grade 4-5)

Table 1

Substance	Sodium Chloride	Water	Copper
Melting Point (°C)	801	0	1083
Boiling Point (°C)	1413	100	2567

3.1   Which substance in **Table 1** would be a liquid at 900 °C?

....

[1]

3.2   Which two substances in **Table 1** would be gases at 1500 °C?

....

[2]

[Total 3 marks]

      Topic C2 — Bonding, Structure and Properties of Matter

Topic C3 — Quantitative Chemistry

Relative Formula Mass

1 The relative atomic mass of chlorine is 35.5. The relative atomic mass of hydrogen is 1. *Grade 3-4*

1.1 Calculate the relative formula mass of hydrochloric acid (HCl).

Relative formula mass = ...
[1]

1.2 Calculate the relative formula mass of chlorine gas (Cl_2).

Relative formula mass = ...
[1]

[Total 2 marks]

2 Match up the following formulas with the correct relative formula mass of the substance. *Grade 4-5*

F_2	38
C_2H_6	40
CaO	30
NaOH	56

[Total 2 marks]

3 Magnesium oxide is a salt with the molecular formula MgO. *Grade 4-5*
Relative atomic masses (A_r): O = 16, Mg = 24

3.1 Calculate the relative formula mass (M_r) of magnesium oxide.

Relative formula mass = ...
[1]

3.2 Calculate the percentage mass of magnesium in magnesium oxide.
Use the equation:

$$\text{Percentage mass of element in a compound} = \frac{A_r \text{ of element} \times \text{number of atoms of element}}{M_r \text{ of compound}} \times 100$$

Percentage mass of magnesium = ... %
[2]

[Total 3 marks]

Conservation of Mass

The word equation for a reaction is shown below.

magnesium $_{(s)}$ + hydrochloric acid $_{(aq)}$ → magnesium chloride $_{(aq)}$ + hydrogen $_{(g)}$

1) Draw circles around the reactants in the equation above.

2) Draw boxes around the products in the equation above.

3) Which of the substances in the reaction is a gas? ....

4) Which of the substances is most likely to escape
   from the reaction container? ....

---

1   Iron and sulfur react together to produce iron sulfide.   Grade 1-3

1.1   Which statement is correct? Tick **one** box.

Some mass will be lost in the reaction.   ☐

The mass of the substances will increase during the reaction.   ☐

The mass of the reactants will be the same as the mass of the products.   ☐

[1]

1.2   28 g of iron reacts with 16 g of sulfur.
How much iron sulfide is made? Tick **one** box.

28 g of iron sulfide. ☐   16 g of iron sulfide. ☐   44 g of iron sulfide. ☐

[1]

[Total 2 marks]

---

2   Sodium hydroxide reacts with hydrochloric acid to produce sodium chloride and water.   Grade 3-4
The equation is: sodium hydroxide + hydrochloric acid → sodium chloride + water

2.1   In an experiment, 80.0 g of sodium hydroxide reacted with 73.0 g of hydrochloric acid.
36.0 g of water was produced. Calculate the mass of sodium chloride produced.

Mass = ... g

[1]

2.2   The experiment was repeated using 109.5 g of hydrochloric acid. 175.5 g of sodium chloride and
54.0 g of water were produced. Calculate the mass of sodium hydroxide that reacted.

Mass = ... g

[1]

[Total 2 marks]

110

3 A student burned 12 g of magnesium in oxygen to produce magnesium oxide.

Grade 4-5

3.1 Which of the following is the correctly balanced equation for the reaction between magnesium and oxygen? Tick **one** box.

$Mg + O \rightarrow MgO$ ☐ $\qquad 2Mg + O_2 \rightarrow 2MgO$ ☐

$Mg + O_2 \rightarrow 2MgO$ ☐ $\qquad Mg + O_2 \rightarrow MgO$ ☐

[1]

3.2 The student measured the mass of magnesium oxide produced. The mass was 20 g. Calculate the mass of oxygen that reacted with the magnesium.

Mass of oxygen = ... g
[1]
[Total 2 marks]

4 A student heated some sodium carbonate powder, as shown in **Figure 1**. When heated, sodium carbonate breaks down to produce sodium oxide and carbon dioxide.

Grade 4-5

The student measured the mass of the reaction container at the start and at the end of the reaction. The measurements the student took are shown in **Figure 2**.

Figure 1

Figure 2

mass at the start of the reaction — 25.4

mass at the end of the reaction — 23.2

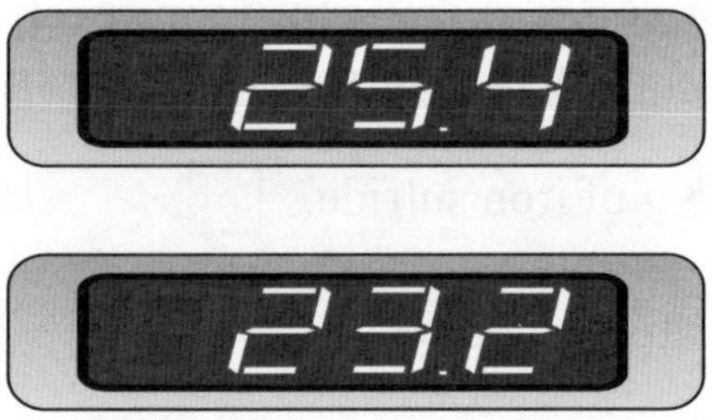

4.1 Calculate the change in mass of the reaction container during the reaction.

Change in mass = ... g
[1]

4.2 The student thinks that the measurements must be wrong, because no mass is lost or gained in a chemical reaction. Is the student correct? Explain your answer.

....

....

....

....

....

[4]
[Total 5 marks]

Concentrations of Solutions

Some units are listed in the table on the right.

Put a tick in the correct column to show whether each unit is a unit of mass or a unit of volume.

Unit	Mass	Volume
g		
cm³		
dm³		
kg		

1 This question is about solutions.

Complete the sentences. Use words from the box.

more	dissolved	less	crystallised	filtered

When a solid is .... in a liquid, a solution is formed.

The greater the mass of the solid, the .... concentrated the solution.

The larger the volume of liquid, the .... concentrated the solution.

[Total 3 marks]

2 28 g of calcium chloride was dissolved in 0.4 dm³ of water.

2.1 Calculate the concentration of the solution and give the units.

Concentration = ... Units = ...
[2]

2.2 Explain the term 'concentration of a solution'.

....

....
[1]

2.3 A student needs another solution of calcium chloride, this time with a concentration of 50 g/dm³. What mass of calcium chloride do they need to add to 0.2 dm³ of water to make this solution?

Mass = ... g
[2]

[Total 5 marks]

Exam Practice Tip

For questions about concentrations, you'll probably need the formula that links concentration, mass and volume. It's a good idea to write down this formula triangle before you start. Then cover up the thing you want to find to work out how to calculate it from the values you do know.

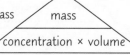

Topic C3 — Quantitative Chemistry

Acids and Bases

1 This question is about acids and bases. **Table 1** shows some everyday substances. *Grade 3-4*

Table 1

Substance	Beer	Bicarbonate of Soda	Milk
pH	4	9	7

1.1 Write the name of the substance in **Table 1** that is an acid.

....

[1]

1.2 What colour would you expect Universal indicator to turn in bicarbonate of soda solution?

....

[1]

[Total 2 marks]

2 The pH of a solution tells you how acidic or alkaline it is. *Grade 4-5*

2.1 Which ion is produced by an acid in aqueous solution? Tick **one** box.

Cl⁻ ☐   H⁺ ☐   OH⁻ ☐   OH⁺ ☐

[1]

2.2 State the range of the pH scale.

....

[2]

[Total 3 marks]

3 Acids and alkalis react together in neutralisation reactions. *Grade 4-5*

3.1 Write the word equation for a neutralisation reaction between an acid and an alkali.

.... + ... → .... + ...

[1]

3.2 Write an equation that shows how hydrogen (H^+) and hydroxide (OH^-) ions react together in a neutralisation reaction.

.... + ... → ....

[1]

3.3 State the pH of the products that form when an acid reacts with an alkali.

....

[1]

[Total 3 marks]

Reactions of Acids

1 Draw **one** line from each acid to the type of salt it forms when it reacts with a base. Grade 1-3

Acid		**Salt**
Hydrochloric acid		Nitrate
Nitric acid		Sulfate
Sulfuric acid		Chloride

[Total 2 marks]

2 Acids react with metal carbonates. Grade 3-4

2.1 Which of the following substances is **not** produced when a metal carbonate reacts with an acid?
Tick **one** box.

Salt ☐   Carbon dioxide ☐   Hydrogen ☐   Water ☐

[1]

2.2 A student adds 2 spatulas of zinc carbonate into a beaker of dilute hydrochloric acid.
The student sees that the reaction fizzes. What product causes the reaction to fizz?

....

[1]

[Total 2 marks]

3 Sulfuric acid reacts with lithium hydroxide to produce lithium sulfate and one other product. Grade 4-5

3.1 Name the product, other than lithium sulfate, that is produced in this reaction.

....

[1]

3.2 Which of the equations below is the balanced symbol equation for the reaction between lithium hydroxide and sulfuric acid?
Tick **one** box.

$2LiOH + H_2SO_4 \rightarrow Li_2SO_4 + 2H_2O$ ☐

$Li_2O + H_2SO_4 \rightarrow Li_2SO_4 + H_2O$ ☐

$Li_2O + H_2SO_4 \rightarrow Li_2SO_4 + H_2$ ☐

$2LiOH + H_2SO_4 \rightarrow Li_2SO_4 + H_2$ ☐

[1]

[Total 2 marks]

Topic C4 — Chemical Changes

4 The salt produced when an acid reacts with a metal hydroxide depends on the reactants.

4.1 Complete **Table 1** to show the salts that are formed when the acids and hydroxides react together.

Table 1

		Acid	
		Hydrochloric acid	Sulfuric acid
Metal hydroxide	Calcium hydroxide	Calcium chloride	....
	Copper hydroxide	....	....
	Magnesium hydroxide	....	....

[2]

4.2 Write a word equation for the reaction between hydrochloric acid and calcium hydroxide.

.... + ... → .... + ...

[1]

4.3 Complete and balance the symbol equation for the reaction between hydrochloric acid and calcium hydroxide.

$Ca(OH)_2$ + ... HCl → .... + 2 ....

[2]

[Total 5 marks]

5 Soluble metal salts can be made from the reactions of acids and metal oxides.

PRACTICAL

5.1 A student makes a soluble salt by reacting zinc oxide with hydrochloric acid.
Name the salt that is produced.

....

[1]

5.2 Write a method that could be used to produce pure crystals of the salt using this reaction.

- Describe how you would make the salt from the reactants.
- Describe how you would purify the salt from the reaction mixture.

....

....

....

....

....

....

....

....

[4]

[Total 5 marks]

The Reactivity Series and Extracting Metals

1   **Figure 1** shows part of the reactivity series of metals. Carbon has also been included in this reactivity series.

Figure 1

Potassium	K
Magnesium	Mg
Carbon	C
Copper	Cu

1.1   Name **one** metal from **Figure 1** that is more reactive than magnesium.

....

[1]

1.2   Name **one** metal from **Figure 1** which could be extracted from its ore by reduction with carbon.

....

[1]

1.3   Which metal in **Figure 1** forms positive ions most easily?

....

[1]

[Total 3 marks]

2   Iron can be extracted from its ore by reduction with carbon. The equation for this reaction is shown below.

$$2Fe_2O_3 + 3C \rightarrow 4Fe + 3CO_2$$

2.1   What is reduction?

....

[1]

2.2   Which element is oxidised in this reaction? Give a reason for your answer.

Element: ....

Reason: ....

[2]

2.3   Explain why magnesium **cannot** be extracted from its ore by reduction with carbon.

....

....

[1]

[Total 4 marks]

Exam Practice Tip

Learning the order of the reactivity series could be really useful when it comes to answering questions in the exams. Try learning this mnemonic to help you remember... <u>P</u>apa <u>S</u>murf <u>L</u>ikes <u>C</u>alling <u>M</u>y <u>C</u>larinet <u>Z</u>any — <u>I</u>sn't <u>H</u>e <u>C</u>ute. (You don't have to use my Booker prize winning version, though. You could also make up your own.)

Topic C4 — Chemical Changes

Reactions of Metals

1 What is the word equation for the reaction of a metal and an acid?
Tick **one** box.

Grade 1-3

metal + acid → salt + water ☐

metal + acid → salt + hydrogen ☐

metal + acid → metal hydroxide + hydrogen ☐

metal + acid → salt + water + hydrogen ☐

[Total 1 mark]

2 A student reacts different metals with water.
The results of this experiment are shown in **Table 1**.

Grade 4-5

Table 1

Reaction	Observation
Copper + water	No reaction
Calcium + water	Fizzing, calcium disappears
Lithium + water	Very vigorous reaction with fizzing, lithium disappears
Magnesium + water	No fizzing, a few bubbles on the magnesium

2.1 Write the word equation for the reaction of calcium and water.

.... + ... → .... + ...

[1]

2.2 Use **Table 1** to put the metals copper, calcium, lithium and magnesium in order of reactivity.

Most reactive .... Least reactive

[2]

2.3 State one thing the student should do to make sure the experiment is fair.

....

[1]

2.4 The student then adds a piece of magnesium to a solution of copper chloride.
A displacement reaction takes place. Predict the products of this reaction.

....

[2]

2.5 State how you can predict whether a displacement reaction will take place between a metal and a metal compound.

....

[1]

[Total 7 marks]

Topic C4 — Chemical Changes

Electrolysis

Place the labels on the correct label lines to identify the parts of an electrochemical cell.

Electrode   Electrolyte

D.C. power supply

1 Electrochemical cells contain electrodes in an electrolyte. The electrolyte can be a liquid or a solution.

Grade 3-4

1.1 Why does the electrolyte need to be a liquid or a solution? Tick **one** box.

So the ions can move to the electrodes ☐

So the electrons can be conducted through the substance ☐

So the electrodes don't corrode ☐

So there is enough heat for the reaction to occur ☐

[1]

1.2 Complete the passage below about electrodes. Use the words in the box. You can use words more than once.

| positive | anode | cathode | gain | negative | lose | neutral |

In electrolysis, the anode is the .... electrode.

.... ions move towards the anode and .... electrons.

The cathode is the .... electrode .

.... ions move towards the cathode and .... electrons.

[6]

[Total 7 marks]

2 Lead bromide can be electrolysed. The electrolyte is molten lead bromide.

Grade 4-5

2.1 What is an electrolyte?

....

[1]

2.2 Write the word equation for the electrolysis of lead bromide.

.... → .... + ...

[1]

[Total 2 marks]

Topic C4 — Chemical Changes

3   **Figure 1** shows the extraction of aluminium. Aluminium oxide is mixed with cryolite. This mixture is then melted and electrolysed. Metallic aluminium is made at the cathode.

Figure 1

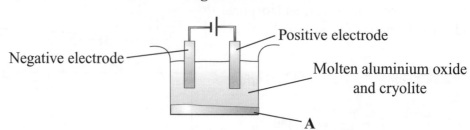

Negative electrode —

Positive electrode

Molten aluminium oxide and cryolite

A

3.1 What is the liquid labelled **A**?

....

[1]

3.2 What is the purpose of mixing the aluminium oxide with cryolite?

....

[1]

3.3 The positive electrode is made of graphite. Why does it need to be replaced regularly?

....

....

[2]

[Total 4 marks]

4   Aqueous iron chloride solution can be electrolysed using inert electrodes. (Grade 4-5)

4.1 Which of the following ions are **not** present in iron chloride solution? Tick **one** box.

☐ Cl^- ☐ Fe^{2+} ☐ OH^- ☐ O^{2-}

[1]

4.2 Explain why hydrogen, not iron, is formed at the cathode.

....

[1]

4.3 State what element is formed at the anode.

....

[1]

[Total 3 marks]

Exam Practice Tip
Remember, when you electrolyse a salt solution, different substances will be formed at the electrodes depending on how reactive they are. If the metal's <u>more</u> reactive than hydrogen, hydrogen will form. If the metal's <u>less</u> reactive than hydrogen, the metal will form. At the anode, water and oxygen will form unless there are halide ions in the solution.

Exothermic and Endothermic Reactions

1 Complete the following definition of an exothermic reaction. Use the words in the box.

Grade
1-3

| takes in | gives out | rise | fall |

An exothermic reaction is one that .... energy.

This is shown by a .... in the temperature of the surroundings.

[Total 2 marks]

2 Chemical reactions result in a transfer of energy.

Grade
3-4

2.1 Compare the amount of energy stored in the products and reactants in an exothermic reaction.

....

[1]

2.2 Which of the following types of reaction is an example of an endothermic reaction?
Tick **one** box.

Combustion ☐   Oxidation ☐   Neutralisation ☐   Thermal decomposition ☐

[1]

[Total 2 marks]

3 During a reaction between solutions of citric acid and sodium hydrogen carbonate, the temperature of the surroundings went down.

Grade
3-4

3.1 How can you tell the reaction is endothermic?

....

[1]

3.2 Where is energy transferred from in an endothermic reaction?

....

[1]

3.3 What happens to the amount of energy in the universe after the reaction?

....

[1]

3.4 Give a practical use of this reaction.

....

[1]

[Total 4 marks]

Exam Practice Tip

The 'en' in 'endothermic' sounds like 'in', and the 'do' is the start of 'down'. So endothermic reactions take energy <u>in</u> from the surroundings, and make the temperature of the surroundings go <u>down</u>. Exothermic reactions do the opposite.

PRACTICAL **Measuring Energy Changes**

1 A student investigated the temperature change of the reaction between sodium hydroxide and hydrochloric acid. The student set up the equipment as shown in **Figure 1**.

Figure 1

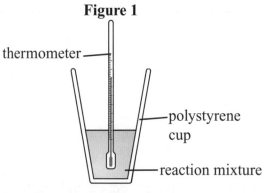

thermometer

polystyrene cup

reaction mixture

1.1 Suggest **one** way the student should change the set-up shown in **Figure 1** in order to make the results more accurate. Give a reason for your answer.

Change: ....

Reason: ....

[2]

1.2 The student carried out the experiment using the method described in the steps below. Write a number 1, 2, 3 or 4 next to each step to put them in the correct order.

Step	Step number
Calculate the temperature change.	....
Mix the reactants together.	....
Measure the temperature of the reactants.	....
Measure the maximum temperature reached by the reaction mixture.	....

[2]

1.3 The results of the experiment are shown in **Table 1**.

Table 1

Initial Temperature (°C)	Final Temperature (°C)
18	31

Calculate the temperature change of the reaction.

Temperature change = ... °C

[1]

1.4 The student repeated the experiment a number of times using a different concentration of acid each time. State the independent and dependent variables in this experiment.

Independent: ....

Dependent: ....

[2]

[Total 7 marks]

Topic C5 — Energy Changes

Reaction Profiles

1 For a reaction to happen, particles need to collide with enough energy.

1.1 What is the name given to the minimum amount of energy needed for a reaction to take place?

....

[1]

1.2 **Figure 1** shows the reaction profile of a reaction.

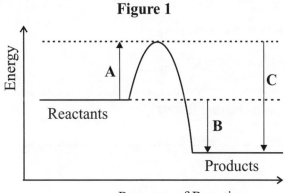

Figure 1

Which letter, **A**, **B**, or **C** shows the amount of energy needed for the reaction to take place?

....

[1]

[Total 2 marks]

2 A reaction profile shows the overall energy change of a reaction.

2.1 **Figure 2** shows the reaction profile for a reaction. Mark the overall energy change on **Figure 2**.

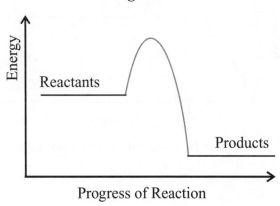

Figure 2

[1]

2.2 What type of reaction is represented by **Figure 2**? Give a reason for your answer.

Type of reaction: ....

Reason: ....

[2]

[Total 3 marks]

Topic C5 — Energy Changes

Rates of Reaction

1   Collision theory can be used to explain the rate of a reaction.

1.1   According to collision theory, what **two** things will cause the rate of a reaction to increase? Tick **two** boxes.

The particles colliding more often.   ☐

The particles colliding less often.   ☐

The particles colliding with more energy.   ☐

The particles colliding with less energy.   ☐

[2]

1.2   At what point in a reaction is the rate fastest?

....

[1]

[Total 3 marks]

2   **Figure 1** shows how the volume of gas produced in a reaction changes over time, for the same reaction under different conditions, **A** and **B**.

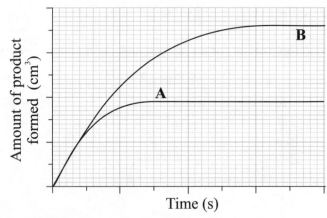

Figure 1

2.1   State whether reaction **A** or reaction **B** produced the most product.

....

[1]

2.2   What does it mean when the graph goes flat?

....

[1]

[Total 2 marks]

Factors Affecting Rates of Reaction

Warm-Up

A student reacts nitric acid with three different forms of calcium carbonate. All other variables are kept the same. Circle the condition that will result in the slowest rate of reaction.

lump of calcium carbonate

calcium carbonate chips

powdered calcium carbonate

1 A scientist carries out a reaction between two gases. **Grade 3-4**

The scientist repeats the experiment but decreases the pressure. All other reaction conditions are kept the same. Complete the paragraph by filling in the gaps. Use the words in the box below.

decrease	more	increase	larger	less	smaller

Decreasing the pressure of the reaction will cause the rate of reaction to ....

This is because the same number of particles are in a .... space, so they will

collide .... frequently.

[Total 3 marks]

2 This question is about the rate of a chemical reaction between two reactants, one of which is in solution, and one of which is a solid. **Grade 4-5**

2.1 Which of the following changes would **not** cause the rate of the chemical reaction to increase?
Tick **one** box.

Increasing the concentration of the solution. ☐

Heating the reaction mixture to a higher temperature. ☐

Using a larger volume of the solution, but keeping the concentration the same. ☐

Grinding the solid reactant so that it forms a fine powder. ☐

[1]

2.2 A catalyst is added to the reaction mixture and all other conditions are kept the same.
The reaction rate increases. Explain why.

....

....

[1]

[Total 2 marks]

PRACTICAL Measuring Rates of Reaction

1 A certain reaction produces a gas product. Which **two** pieces of equipment below could be used to monitor the rate at which the gas is produced? Tick **two** boxes.

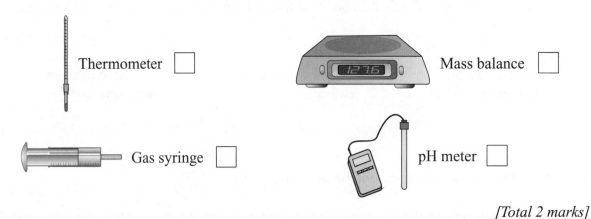

Thermometer ☐

Mass balance ☐

Gas syringe ☐

pH meter ☐

[Total 2 marks]

2 A student measures the volume of gas produced by the reaction between sulfuric acid and marble chips. He repeats the experiment with two different concentrations of acid, **A** and **B**. **Table 1** shows his results.

Table 1

		Time (s)					
		0	10	20	30	40	50
Volume of gas produced (cm³)	Concentration A	3	8	10	12	16	19
	Concentration B	9	19	25	29	32	35

2.1 State the concentration, **A** or **B**, which resulted in the fastest reaction.
Give a reason for your answer.

Concentration: ....

Reason: ....

....

[2]

2.2 What are the dependent and independent variables in this experiment?

Dependent variable: ....

Independent variable: ....

[2]

2.3 Suggest **one** variable that would have to be controlled in this experiment to make it a fair test.

....

[1]

[Total 5 marks]

Topic C6 — The Rate and Extent of Chemical Change

More on Measuring Rates PRACTICAL

1 A student carries out a reaction in a conical flask. She measures the time it takes for a black cross placed under the flask to disappear as a precipitate is formed. Under different conditions, the rate of the reaction changes.

Grade 3-4

Complete the sentences below. Use words from the box.

| more quickly   more slowly   in the same time |

If the rate is higher than the rate of the original reaction,

the cross will disappear ....

If the rate is lower than the rate of the original reaction,

the cross will disappear ....

[Total 2 marks]

2 A student investigates how the concentration of acid affects the rate of reaction between hydrochloric acid and sodium thiosulfate. The reaction forms a yellow precipitate. Her experimental set up is shown in **Figure 1**.

 Grade 4-5

Figure 1

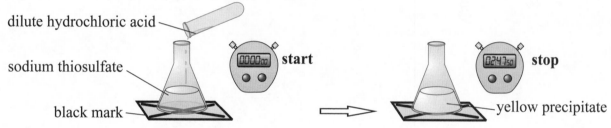

dilute hydrochloric acid

sodium thiosulfate

black mark

start

stop

yellow precipitate

She uses five different acid concentrations and records how long it takes for the mark to disappear. All other variables are kept the same. Some of her results are shown in **Table 1**.

Table 1

Concentration of hydrochloric acid (g/dm³)	15	30	45	....	75
Time taken for mark to disappear (s)	....	187	....	174	168

2.1 Use the answers from the box below to complete **Table 1**.

| 90   181   165   60   194 |

[3]

2.2 Another student was observing these reactions but got different results to the first student. Suggest **one** reason why they may have different results.

....

[1]

[Total 4 marks]

Topic C6 — The Rate and Extent of Chemical Change

Graphs of Reaction Rate Experiments

1   The rate of a reaction was investigated by measuring the volume of gas produced at regular intervals. The results are shown in **Table 1**.

Table 1

Time (s)	0	50	100	150	200	250	300
Volume of gas (cm³)	0.0	9.5	14.5	16.0	16.5	16.5	16.5

1.1 Plot the data in **Table 1** on the axes below. Draw a curved line of best fit onto the graph.

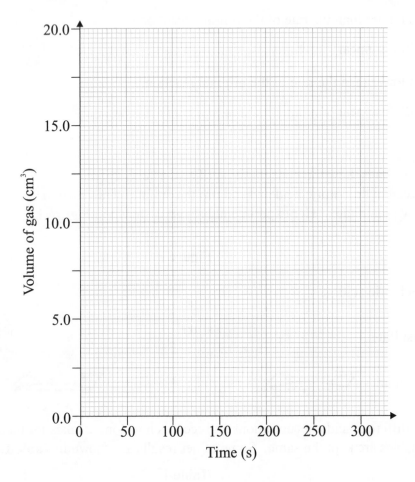

[3]

1.2 Draw tangents to the graph at 75 seconds and at 175 seconds.

[2]

1.3 Using the tangents drawn in part 1.2, state whether the reaction is fastest at 75 s or at 175 s. Give a reason for your answer.

Time: ....

Reason: ....

[2]

[Total 7 marks]

Exam Practice Tip

Plotting graphs can sometimes take a while, but make sure you take your time. It's easy to miss out a point or plot an x-value with the wrong y-value. You might be given a graph which doesn't have many values on the axis (like the graph's y-axis on this page). If so, feel free to add more values or markers to make it quicker and easier to plot your graph.

Topic C6 — The Rate and Extent of Chemical Change

Working Out Reaction Rates

1   In a reaction that lasted 125 seconds, 40 cm³ of gas was produced.   **Grade 3-4**

1.1   Calculate the mean rate of the reaction.   Use the equation:

$$\text{mean rate of reaction} = \frac{\text{amount of product formed}}{\text{time}}$$

.... units

[2]

1.2   What will the units of the rate be?   Tick **one** box.

s/cm³ ☐   cm³/s ☐   s³/cm ☐   cm/s³ ☐

[1]

[Total 3 marks]

2   **Figure 1** shows the volume of hydrogen gas produced during a reaction between magnesium and hydrochloric acid.   **Grade 4-5**

Figure 1

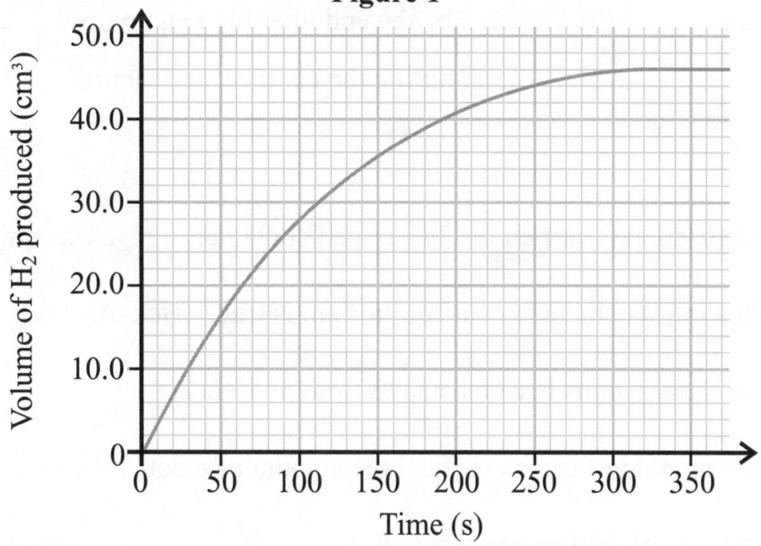

2.1   Calculate the mean rate for the whole reaction.   Give your answer to 3 significant figures.
Use **Figure 1** and the equation:

$$\text{mean rate of reaction} = \frac{\text{amount of product formed}}{\text{time}}$$

.... cm³/s

[2]

2.2   Calculate the mean rate of reaction between 100 seconds and 250 seconds.
Give your answer to 3 significant figures.

.... cm³/s

[4]

[Total 6 marks]

Topic C6 — The Rate and Extent of Chemical Change

Reversible Reactions

1 Choose the symbol below that is used in a reaction equation to show that the reaction is reversible. Tick **one** box.

Grade 1-3

$\rightleftharpoons$ ☐ $\rightleftarrows$ ☐ $\Leftrightarrow$ ☐ $\leftrightarrow$ ☐

[Total 1 mark]

2 The two sentences below describe a reversible reaction. The forward reaction is endothermic and the backward reaction is exothermic. Complete the two sentences.

Grade 3-4

Use answers from the box.

taken in	products	given out	the same as	reactants	different to

1 When the reaction is cooled, it moves in the forward direction

and the amount of .... increases.

2 The energy .... by the endothermic reaction is ....

the amount .... during the exothermic reaction.

[Total 4 marks]

3 When a reversible reaction is carried out in a sealed container, it reaches equilibrium.

Grade 4-5

3.1 Which of the following statements about equilibrium is true? Tick **one** box.

At equilibrium, all the reactants have reacted to form products. ☐

At equilibrium, the amount of products equal the amount of reactants. ☐

At equilibrium, the rate of the forward reaction
is equal to the rate of the backwards reaction. ☐

At equilibrium, both the forwards and the backwards reactions stop. ☐

[1]

3.2 The sealed container is an example of a 'closed system'. Explain what this term means.

....

....

[1]

[Total 2 marks]

Exam Practice Tip

When a reaction's at equilibrium, if there are more products than reactants, the reaction is going in the forwards direction. If there are more reactants than products at equilibrium, it's going in the backwards direction. But remember, the forward and backward reactions are going at the same rate and the amounts of products and reactants don't change.

Topic C6 — The Rate and Extent of Chemical Change

Hydrocarbons

1 The names of three alkanes (labelled **A**, **B** and **C**) are given below. **Figure 1** shows an alkane.

Grade 1-3

Figure 1

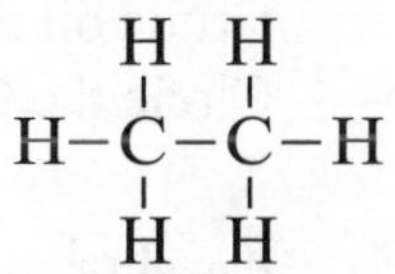

$$H-\underset{\underset{H}{|}}{\overset{\overset{H}{|}}{C}}-\underset{\underset{H}{|}}{\overset{\overset{H}{|}}{C}}-H$$

  A ethane   **B** propane   **C** methane

1.1 What is the name of the alkane shown in **Figure 1**?
Write the letter **A**, **B** or **C** in the box.

☐

[1]

1.2 Which alkane contains three carbon atoms?
Write the letter **A**, **B** or **C** in the box.

☐

[1]

[Total 2 marks]

2 Alkanes are a family of hydrocarbons.   Grade 3-4

2.1 What is a hydrocarbon?

....

[2]

2.2 Complete the word equation for the complete combustion of an alkane.

    alkane + oxygen → .... + ...

[1]

2.3 During a combustion reaction, the atoms in the alkane gain oxygen.
What is the name of this process?

....

[1]

[Total 4 marks]

3 The molecular formulas for five hydrocarbons, **A** to **E**, are shown below.   Grade 4-5

  A C_4H_8 **B** C_4H_{10} **C** C_5H_{10} **D** C_5H_{12} **E** C_3H_8

3.1 Which of the hydrocarbons are alkanes? Explain your answer.

....

....

[2]

3.2 What is the name of hydrocarbon **B**?

....

[1]

3.3 Hydrocarbon **D** can be burned in air. Balance the equation for this reaction.

$$C_5H_{12} \ + \ .... \ O_2 \ \rightarrow \ .... \ CO_2 \ + \ .... \ H_2O$$

[3]

[Total 6 marks]

Crude Oil

Warm-Up

Crude oil is used to make fuels for transport.
Circle the **four** substances below that are fuels made from crude oil.

diesel oil   petrol   kerosene   plastic

plankton   liquefied petroleum gas   oxygen   metal ores

1   This question is about crude oil.   (Grade 3-4)

1.1   Complete the sentences below. Use words from the box.

mud	finite	organic	renewable	plankton

Crude oil is formed from .... and the remains of other plants and animals

that were buried in .... millions of years ago. Crude oil is being used up

much more quickly than it's being made, so it's a .... resource.

[3]

1.2   Substances made from crude oil are useful as fuels.
Give **two other** useful products that can be made from crude oil.

1 ....

2 ....

[2]

[Total 5 marks]

2   Crude oil is a resource that contains hydrocarbons.   (Grade 4-5)

2.1   What property of hydrocarbons means that a large number of
different products can be made from crude oil? Tick **one** box.

Carbon can bond to all of the elements in the periodic table. ☐

Hydrogen atoms can bond with each other to form chains and rings. ☐

Carbon atoms bond together to form different groups of compounds. ☐

[1]

2.2   Different hydrocarbons have carbon chains of different lengths.
How does the boiling point of hydrocarbons change as the length of their carbon chains increases?

....

[1]

2.3   State **one** property of hydrocarbons, other than boiling point,
that changes as the length of the carbon chain increases.

....

[1]

[Total 3 marks]

Fractional Distillation

1   **Figure 1** shows a fractionating column.
They are used in the fractional distillation of crude oil.

Grade 1-3

Figure 1

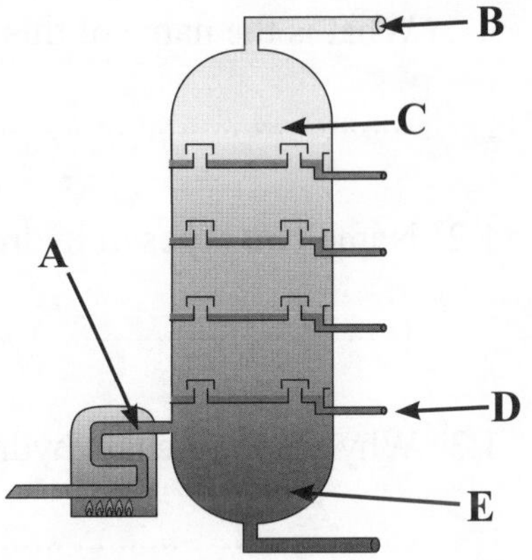

1.1   Where does crude oil enter the fractionating column?
Tick **one** box.

A ☐   B ☐   C ☐   D ☐   E ☐

[1]

1.2   Which is the hottest part of the fractionating column?
Tick **one** box.

A ☐   B ☐   C ☐   D ☐   E ☐

[1]

1.3   Where do the shortest hydrocarbons leave the fractionating column?
Tick **one** box.

A ☐   B ☐   C ☐   D ☐   E ☐

[1]

[Total 3 marks]

2   Before it enters the fractionating column, crude oil is heated until most of it evaporates.

Grade 4-5

2.1   What change of state happens to the evaporated crude oil within the fractionating column?
Explain why this happens.

Change of state: ....

Explanation: ....

....

[2]

2.2* In fractional distillation of crude oil, the hydrocarbons are separated out
depending on the length of their carbon chains. Explain how this happens.

....

....

....

....

....

....

....

....

[6]

[Total 8 marks]

Exam Practice Tip

It's important to understand how a fractionating column works and why different substances drain out at different points.

 ☐   ☐   ☐

Cracking

1 Crude oil is processed to make a variety of different products. *Grade 3-4*

1.1 Long-chain hydrocarbons can be processed to produce short-chain hydrocarbons. What is the name of this process?

....

[1]

1.2 Name **two** types of hydrocarbons that are produced as a result of this process.

1 .... 2 ....

[2]

1.3 Why are long-chain hydrocarbons broken into shorter chain hydrocarbons?

....

[1]

[Total 4 marks]

2 Catalytic cracking and steam cracking can both be used to crack hydrocarbons. *Grade 4-5*

2.1 Describe the method for steam cracking.

....

....

[2]

2.2 State one way in which the method for catalytic cracking is different to steam cracking.

....

[1]

2.3 Dodecane is an alkane with the formula $C_{12}H_{26}$. It can be cracked to produce heptane (C_7H_{16}) and one other hydrocarbon. Give the formula of this other hydrocarbon.

....

[1]

2.4 Dodecane can also be cracked to produce hexane (C_6H_{14}) and one other hydrocarbon. Balance the equation for cracking dodecane.

$$C_{12}H_{26} \quad \rightarrow \quad C_6H_{14} \quad + \quad 2C\text{.....}H\text{.......}$$

[2]

2.5 A scientist has a sample of hexane (an alkane) and a sample of pentene (an alkene). Describe a test that can be used to identify which sample is pentene. Include the test results that you would expect the scientist to see.

....

....

....

....

[3]

[Total 9 marks]

Topic C7 — Organic Chemistry

Purity and Formulations

1 A paint was made up of 20% pigment, 35% binder, 25% solvent, and 20% additives. *(Grade 3-4)*

1.1 Which of the statements below does **not** explain why the paint is a formulation? Tick **one** box.

It is a mixture that has been designed for a certain use. ☐

Each part contributes to the properties of the formulation. ☐

The mixture is made up of less than five parts. ☐

Each part of the mixture is present in a measured amount. ☐

[1]

1.2 Other than paint, name **one** example of a formulation.

....

[1]

[Total 2 marks]

2 This question is about purity. *(Grade 4-5)*

2.1 How is a pure substance defined in chemistry? Tick **one** box.

A single element not mixed with any other substance. ☐

A single compound not mixed with any other substance. ☐

A single element or compound not mixed with any other substance. ☐

An element that has not been reacted with anything. ☐

[1]

2.2 The melting point of two samples of copper were measured. Sample **A** had a melting point of 1085 °C and sample **B** melted over the range 900 – 940 °C. Suggest which of the two samples was pure. Explain your answer.

....

....

[2]

2.3 The boiling point of water is 100 °C.
A scientist adds some salt to a sample of water and measures the boiling point of the solution. How will the addition of salt affect the boiling point of the water?

....

[1]

[Total 4 marks]

Exam Practice Tip

A formulation is a mixture but a mixture isn't always a formulation. For the exam make sure you know what the difference is. Formulations are designed for a particular use and contain ingredients in specific amounts.

 ☐   ☐   ☐

134

Paper Chromatography

Use the words to label the different parts of the
chromatography experiment shown on the right.

baseline   filter paper   ....

spots of chemicals   ....

solvent front

1   Paper chromatograms were produced for three dyes, **D**, **E** and **F**, using different solvents.
Figure 1 shows a chromatogram produced using ethanol as the solvent.

Figure 1

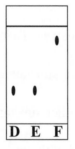

D E F

1.1 The chromatography experiment that produced the chromatogram in **Figure 1** had two phases.
Which of the following statements describing the mobile phase is **true**? Tick **one** box.

The dyes moved in the mobile phase. ☐

The mobile phase was the filter paper. ☐

The stationary phase moved up the mobile phase. ☐

The least soluble dye spent a longer time in the mobile phase. ☐

[1]

1.2 Why do different substances travel different distances along the paper?

....

....

[1]

1.3 In all solvents, each dye only has one spot. What does this suggest about the dyes?

....

[1]

[Total 3 marks]

Topic C8 — Chemical Analysis

Using Chromatograms

1   A scientist used chromatography to analyse the composition of five food colourings. Four of the colourings were unknown (**A** – **D**). The other was sunrise yellow. The results are shown in **Figure 1**.

Figure 1

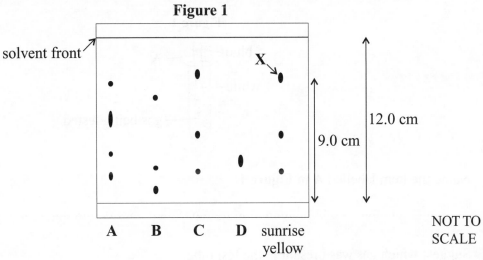

solvent front

X

12.0 cm

9.0 cm

A   B   C   D   sunrise yellow

NOT TO SCALE

1.1 Which food colouring definitely contains at least four different substances?

....

[1]

1.2 Which of the food colourings, **A-D**, could be made of the same substances as sunrise yellow?

....

[1]

1.3 How could you check whether the food colouring you identified in question 1.2 is made of the same substances as sunrise yellow?

....

....

....

[2]

1.4 Calculate the R_f value for the spot of chemical labelled **X** in **Figure 1**.

Use the equation: $R_f = \dfrac{\text{distance moved by substance}}{\text{distance moved by solvent}}$

R_f = ...

[2]

1.5 Describe how the scientist could use chromatography to find out whether food colouring **A** contained a particular substance.

....

....

....

[2]

[Total 8 marks]

Tests for Gases

1 A student wants to identify a gaseous product.

Figure 1 shows the gas being tested.

Figure 1

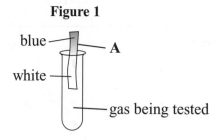

blue —— A
white ——
—— gas being tested

1.1 Name the item labelled **A** in **Figure 1**.

....

[1]

1.2 Suggest which gas was present in the test tube.

....

[1]

[Total 2 marks]

2 A student performs an experiment that produces a colourless gas. To identify the gas, she collects it and carries out tests.

2.1 Suggest why the student should perform the experiment in a fume cupboard.

....

[1]

2.2 The student bubbles some of the gas through limewater. What gas is this test used to identify?

....

[1]

2.3 When a lighted splint was placed into a sample of the gas, it was **not** accompanied by a popping sound. What does this tell you about the gas?

....

[1]

2.4 When the student placed a glowing splint into a sample of the gas, the splint relighted. Name the gas that was produced by her experiment.

....

[1]

[Total 4 marks]

Topic C8 — Chemical Analysis

The Evolution of the Atmosphere

Warm-Up

Write the numbers 1-4 in the boxes below to put the events in the order in which they happened.

Animals evolved. ☐   The oceans formed. ☐

The early atmosphere formed. ☐   Plants evolved. ☐

1   The composition of gases in the atmosphere has varied during Earth's history. (Grade 3-4)

   1.1   What are the approximate proportions of oxygen and nitrogen in the atmosphere today?
Tick **one** box.

     Four-fifths oxygen and one-fifth nitrogen. ☐   Three-fifths oxygen and two-fifths nitrogen. ☐

     One-fifth oxygen and four-fifths nitrogen. ☐   Two-fifths oxygen and three-fifths nitrogen. ☐

[1]

   1.2   Other than oxygen and nitrogen, name **two** gases in the atmosphere today.

     ....

[2]

   1.3   How was the oxygen in the atmosphere produced?

     ....

[1]

   1.4   How was nitrogen in the atmosphere produced?

     ....

[1]

[Total 5 marks]

2*   Describe how the amount of carbon dioxide in the atmosphere got to the level that it is at today. (Grade 4-5)

Include ideas about:
- How carbon dioxide originally became part of the atmosphere.
- How the amount of carbon dioxide in the early atmosphere was different to how it is today.
- Reasons why the amount of atmospheric carbon dioxide has changed.

....

....

....

....

....

....

....

....

[Total 6 marks]

 ☐   ☐   ☐

Greenhouse Gases and Climate Change

1 Greenhouse gases in the atmosphere help maintain life on Earth. *(Grade 4-5)*

1.1 Which of the following is **not** a greenhouse gas? Tick **one** box.

Nitrogen ☐   Carbon dioxide ☐   Water vapour ☐   Methane ☐

[1]

1.2 Use the words in the box below to complete the paragraph describing the greenhouse effect.

long	absorbed	cools	short	reflected	warms

The sun gives out .... wavelength radiation.

The Earth reflects this as .... wavelength radiation.

This radiation is .... by greenhouse gases and then given out in all directions.

Some heads back to Earth and .... the Earth's surface.

[4]

[Total 5 marks]

2 **Figure 1** shows how the concentration of CO_2 in the atmosphere has changed over time. *(Grade 4-5)*

Figure 1

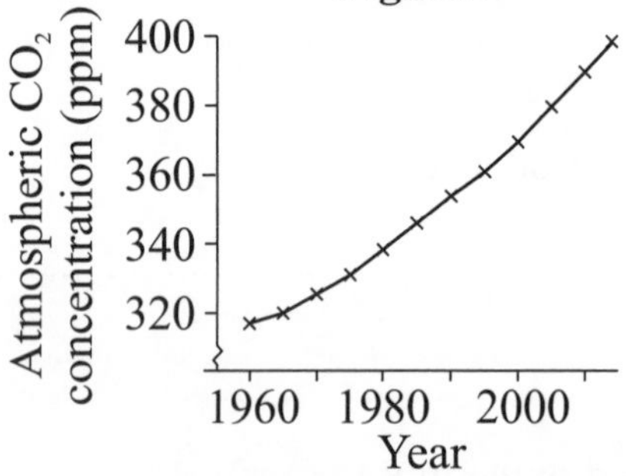

2.1 Outline what **Figure 1** tells you about the concentration of atmospheric carbon dioxide.

....

....

[1]

2.2 Give **one** example of a type of human activity which has contributed to the change in atmospheric carbon dioxide concentration, shown in **Figure 1**.

....

[1]

2.3 Over the same time period, the global temperature has increased. Suggest **one** reason why it's hard to prove that the change in carbon dioxide is causing the increase in temperature.

....

[1]

2.4 Increased global temperature could cause climate change. Give **one** possible effect of climate change.

....

[1]

[Total 4 marks]

Carbon Footprints

1   In recent years, governments and businesses have tried to reduce their carbon footprints.   Grade 3-4

1.1   The following statements describe some of the difficulties in reducing carbon footprints.
Which of the statements is **false**? Tick **one** box.

Governments are worried that their economies will
be affected if they try to reduce carbon footprints.   ☐

Countries cannot always make agreements about reducing emissions.   ☐

Governments are worried that reducing carbon
footprints could lead to sea levels rising.   ☐

Technologies with lower carbon footprints need more development.   ☐

[1]

1.2   Complete **Table 1** to show whether each action would increase or decrease a carbon footprint.
Tick **one** box in each row.

Table 1

Action	Increase	Decrease
Producing more waste		
Using more renewable energy resources		
Using more fossil fuels		
Using processes that require more energy		
Capturing carbon dioxide and storing it underground		

[3]

[Total 4 marks]

2   Individuals have an annual carbon footprint.   Grade 4-5

2.1   What is meant by the term 'carbon footprint'?

....

....

[2]

2.2   Suggest **two** reasons why an individual may not try to reduce their carbon footprint.

....

....

[2]

[Total 4 marks]

Exam Practice Tip

Learning the definitions for all the different terms that crop up in GCSE Science may be a bit of a bore, but it might be
really useful in the exams. Learning all the itty bitty details is worth it if it means you get all the marks available.

      Topic C9 — Chemistry of the Atmosphere

Air Pollution

1 Draw **one** line from each pollutant to show how it's formed.

Pollutant	**How Pollutant is Formed**

sulfur dioxide

Incomplete combustion of hydrocarbons.

nitrogen oxides

Reaction of gases in the air caused by the heat of burning fossil fuels.

particulates

Combustion of fossil fuels that contain sulfur impurities.

[Total 2 marks]

2 Some of the pollutants that are released when fuels burn can cause acid rain.

2.1 Name **one** pollutant that can lead to acid rain.

....

[1]

2.2 State **two** ways in which acid rain can be damaging.

....

....

[2]

[Total 3 marks]

3 Combustion of fuel in cars is a major contributor to air pollution.

3.1 Nitrogen oxides can be formed from the combustion of fuels in cars.
Give **two** problems caused by nitrogen oxides in the environment.

....

....

[2]

3.2 Fuel combustion can produce particulates. What impact do particulates have on human health?

....

[1]

3.3 Combustion of fuels can also produce a gas that prevents blood from carrying oxygen
around the body. Inhaling it can cause health problems, and sometimes death.

Name the gas and give the reason why it is difficult to detect it.

Name: ....

Reason: ....

[2]

[Total 5 marks]

Topic C9 — Chemistry of the Atmosphere

Finite and Renewable Resources

1   This question is about sustainable use of the Earth's resources.
    Table 1 shows the time it takes to form various materials.

Table 1

Material	Time to form (years)
Wood	2-20
Coal	3×10^8
Cotton	0.5

1.1 Using the data in **Table 1**, state **one** finite resource. Explain your answer.

Resource: ....

Reason: ....

[2]

1.2 What is meant by the term 'renewable resource'?

....

[1]

1.3 Name **one** other renewable resource that is not listed in **Table 1**.

....

[1]

[Total 4 marks]

2   Humans have developed items made from both natural and synthetic materials.

2.1 Give **one** example of how agriculture is used to increase the supply of a natural resource.

....

....

[1]

2.2 Give **one** example of a synthetic product which has replaced
     or is used in addition to a natural resource.

....

[1]

[Total 2 marks]

Exam Practice Tip

If numbers are really big or small, they could be given in standard form, like the time taken for coal to form in Table 1
(3×10^8). You can tell how big the number is by looking at the little number next to the 10. If the little number is
positive, then the whole number is greater than 1. The higher this little number is, the bigger the whole number will be.
If the little number is negative, it means the whole number is between 0 and 1. The more negative this little number is,
the smaller the whole number will be. Give this a read a few times until it makes sense.

Reuse and Recycling

1 Some materials can be recycled into new products. (Grade 3-4)

1.1 Which of the following statements about the recycling of metals is **false**? Tick **one** box.

Recycling metals reduces the amount of waste sent to landfill. ☐

Recycling metals can increase the finite amount of some metals in the Earth. ☐

Recycling metals often uses less energy than making new metals. ☐

Recycling metals saves some of the finite amount of metals in the Earth. ☐

[1]

1.2 Glass can be recycled and made into new products.
Using the words in the box, complete the sentences below.

melted	reshaped	less	crushed	more

Glass products are .... and then ....

They are then .... to make other products for a different use.

This process uses .... energy than making new glass.

[4]

[Total 5 marks]

2 Cups and mugs for hot drinks can be made from different materials.
Two possible materials are stainless steel and paper.
Table 1 gives some information about these materials. (Grade 4-5)

Table 1

	Stainless Steel Mug	Paper Cup
Source of raw material	Metal ores and coal	Plant fibre
Can it be reused or recycled?	Both	Possible but not widely done.

2.1 Using the information in **Table 1**, state which of the two raw materials is more sustainable.
Give a reason for your answer.

Raw material: ....

Reason: ....

[2]

2.2 The stainless steel mug can be reused many times.
Suggest why this may make it more sustainable than the paper cup.

....

....

[1]

[Total 3 marks]

Life Cycle Assessments

Draw one line between each stage of a product's life and the correct example of that stage.

Life cycle stage	Example
Getting the Raw Materials	Coal being mined from the ground.
Manufacturing and Packaging	Plastic bags going to landfill.
Using the Product	A car using fuel while driving.
Product Disposal	Books being made from wood pulp.

1 What is the purpose of a life cycle assessment? Tick **one** box. (Grade 1-3)

It looks at how many different chemicals are used during the life cycle of a product. ☐

It looks at the total amount of greenhouse gases produced during the life cycle of a product. ☐

It looks at every stage of a product's life to assess the impact on the environment. ☐

It looks at the total economic impact of each stage of a product's life. ☐

[Total 1 mark]

2 A mobile phone company is carrying out a life cycle assessment for one of their products. (Grade 3-4)

2.1 Suggest **one** environmental problem associated with using metals as a raw material.

....

[1]

2.2 The mobile phone is powered by a battery which needs to be recharged regularly. Most electricity comes from burning fossil fuels. Suggest **one** environmental problem that this may cause.

....

[1]

2.3 Mobile phones can be recycled. However, some still get sent to landfill.
Give **two** disadvantages of disposing of rubbish in landfill.

1 ....

2 ....

[2]

[Total 4 marks]

 ☐ ☐ ☐

Topic C10 — Using Resources

Using Life Cycle Assessments

1 A company carries out a life cycle assessment (LCA) for a new product. The LCA only shows some of the environmental impacts that are caused by the product. How can this type of LCA be described? Tick **one** box.

Grade 1-3

limited life cycle assessment ☐

selective life cycle assessment ☐

incomplete life cycle assessment ☐

exclusive life cycle assessment ☐

[Total 1 mark]

2 A new shop is deciding whether to stock plastic bags or paper bags for their customers' shopping. To help them decide, they carry out a life cycle assessment for each type of bag. Some information about each bag is shown in **Table 1**.

Grade 4-5

Table 1

	Plastic bag	**Paper bag**
Raw materials	Crude oil	Wood
Manufacture	A little waste produced.	Lots of waste produced.
Using the product	Can be reused several times.	Usually only used once.
Disposal	Recyclable Not biodegradable	Recyclable Biodegradable

2.1 Using the information in **Table 1**, give **two** advantages of plastic bags over paper bags.

1 ....

2 ....

[2]

2.2 Suggest **two** other pieces of information, that are not given in **Table 1**, that would be needed to help decide which bag has the least impact on the environment.

1 ....

2 ....

[2]

[Total 4 marks]

Potable Water

Circle the words below which are sources of surface water.

sewage   reservoirs   lakes

                                                    oceans

        rivers   underground rocks   seas

---

1   This question is about potable water.   Grade 3-4

1.1   Which of the following is a correct description of potable water? Tick **one** box.

Pure water ☐

Water with a pH between 4.5 and 6.5 ☐

Water that is safe to drink ☐

Water with a high concentration of salt ☐

[1]

1.2   In the warmer areas of the UK, surface water can dry up. Suggest a suitable source
of fresh water that could be used instead for the production of potable water.

....

[1]

[Total 2 marks]

---

2   Fresh water needs to be treated before it is safe to drink.   Grade 4-5

2.1   Draw **one** line between each treatment of water and the substances removed by the process.

| Passing water through filter beds | | Solid Waste |

| | Microbes |

| Sterilisation | | Chemicals |

[2]

2.2   Name **three** things that can be used to sterilise fresh water.

1   ....

2   ....

3   ....

[3]

[Total 5 marks]

Desalination

1 **Figure 1** shows a set of equipment that could be used to desalinate sea water through a process known as distillation.

Figure 1

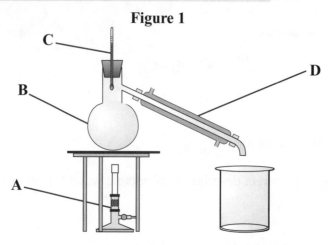

Name the components labelled **A** to **D** in **Figure 1**. Use the words in the box.

round bottomed flask	condenser	thermometer	Bunsen burner

A ....   B ....

C ....   D ....

[Total 4 marks]

2 Before seawater can be used for drinking water, it needs to go through desalination. Desalination is the process of removing salts.

2.1 Reverse osmosis is a type of desalination that uses membranes. Which of the following statements describes how membranes help to purify seawater? Tick **one** box.

The membranes let salt molecules pass through but stop the water from passing. ☐

The membranes let water molecules pass through but trap the salts. ☐

The salt molecules stick to the membranes which are then removed from the water. ☐

The membranes heat the water causing it to evaporate. ☐

[1]

2.2 Although it is surrounded by the sea, the UK produces potable water from fresh water sources, rather than from sea water. Explain why the UK chooses to use fresh water sources.

....

....

[2]

[Total 3 marks]

Exam Practice Tip

Some water costs a lot to make potable, some not so much. Make sure you understand the different processes that salty water and fresh water undergo to make it safe to drink and why the different processes are used in different places.

Waste Water Treatment

1   Waste water must be treated before being reused or released into the environment.   *Grade 3-4*

1.1 Which **two** of the following pollutants must be removed
from sewage and agricultural waste water? Tick **two** boxes.

Calcium ions, Ca^{2+} ☐

Organic matter ☐

Harmful microbes ☐

Sodium ions, Na^+ ☐

[2]

1.2 Industrial waste water sometimes needs further treatment compared to
sewage and agricultural waste water. Suggest why this.

....

[1]

[Total 3 marks]

2   This question is about the treatment of waste water in the form of sewage.
Figure 1 shows the different stages water goes through at a sewage treatment facility.   *Grade 4-5*

Figure 1

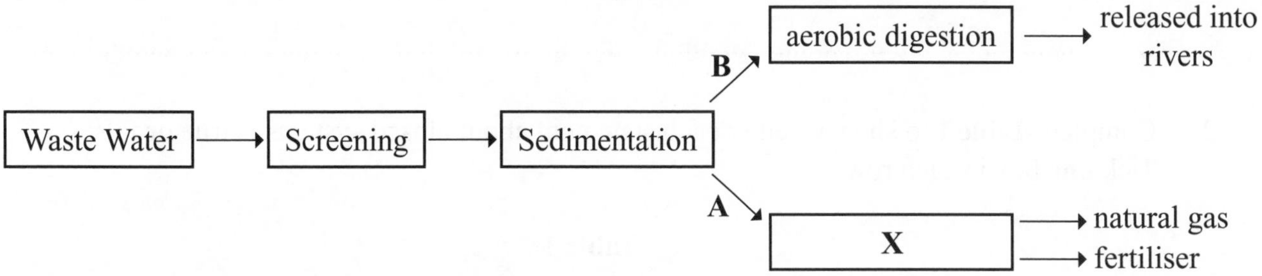

2.1 What is the purpose of the stage described as 'screening'?

....

....

[2]

2.2 What are the names given to the two substances produced by sedimentation?

Substance **A**: ....

Substance **B**: ....

[2]

2.3 What is the name of process **X**?

....

[1]

[Total 5 marks]

Topic C10 — Using Resources

Topic P1 — Energy

Energy Stores and Systems

1 Draw **one** straight line from each object to the energy store that energy is being transferred **from**.

Object	Energy store
A car slowing down without braking.	chemical energy store
A mug of hot tea cooling down.	thermal energy store
A stretched spring returning to its original shape.	elastic potential energy store
A battery in a circuit.	kinetic energy store

[Total 3 marks]

2 Whenever a system changes, energy is transferred.

2.1 Define the term 'system'.

....

[1]

2.2 Complete **Table 1** to show whether each statement about closed systems is true or false. Tick **one** box in each row.

Table 1

Statement	True	False
Energy can only be transferred mechanically or electrically in a closed system.		
A closed system is one in which there is no net change in the system's total energy.		
Energy can be transferred into and out of a closed system.		

[3]

[Total 4 marks]

Exam Practice Tip

Make sure you know the different types of energy store. Remember that energy can be transferred between stores mechanically (because of a force doing work), electrically, by heating or by radiation (e.g. light and sound waves).

Conservation of Energy and Energy Transfers

1 Which statements about energy are **false**? Tick **two** boxes. *(Grade 1-3)*

Energy can be transferred usefully. ☐

Energy can be created. ☐

Energy can be stored. ☐

Energy can be dissipated. ☐

Energy can be destroyed. ☐

[Total 2 marks]

2 An apple is hanging from a branch of a tree. *(Grade 3-4)*

2.1 The apple falls from the tree.
Give the **two** energy stores that energy is transferred between as the apple is falling.
You can assume there is no air resistance.

Energy is transferred from: ....

Energy is transferred to: ....

[2]

2.2 The passage below describes what is happening as the apple falls.
Use words from the box below to complete the passage.

electrostatic	mechanically	gravitational
work		energy

As the apple falls, ... is done on the apple by the

.... force. This means energy is transferred ....

[3]

[Total 5 marks]

3 A cyclist on a road applies his brakes to come to a stop.
Applying the brakes causes the brakes to warm up. *(Grade 4-5)*

Describe the energy transfer that has occurred.
You can ignore any friction between the bike and the ground.
You can also assume there is no air resistance.

....

....

....

[Total 3 marks]

Topic P1 — Energy

Kinetic and Potential Energy Stores

1 A student stretches a spring by 0.01 m.
The spring is not stretched past its limit of proportionality.
The spring has a spring constant of 20 N/m.

Calculate the energy stored in the elastic potential energy store of the spring as it is stretched.
Use an equation from the Equations List.

Energy = ... J

[Total 2 marks]

2 A girl kicks a ball resting on the ground into the air.
The ball reaches a height of 2.0 m. The ball has a mass of 0.50 kg.
Gravitational field strength = 9.8 N/kg.

2.1 Write down the equation that links the energy in an object's gravitational potential energy store, the mass of the object, gravitational field strength and height.

....

[1]

2.2 Calculate the energy transferred to the ball's gravitational potential energy store.

Energy = ... J

[2]

2.3 The ball falls back down to the ground. All of the energy stored in the ball's gravitational potential energy store is transferred to its kinetic energy store.
Calculate the speed of the ball when it hits the ground.
Give your answer to 2 significant figures.
Use the equation:

$$\text{kinetic energy} = \frac{1}{2} \times \text{mass} \times (\text{speed})^2$$

Speed = ... m/s

[3]

[Total 6 marks]

Energy Transfers by Heating

Which of the following is the correct definition of specific heat capacity? Tick **one** box.

The energy transferred when an object is burnt. ☐

The maximum amount of energy an object can store before it melts. ☐

The energy needed to raise the temperature of 1 kg of a substance by 10 °C. ☐

The energy needed to raise the temperature of 1 kg of a substance by 1 °C. ☐

---

1 Use phrases from the box below to complete the passage. *(Grade 3-4)*

thermal	kinetic	electrically	mechanically	by heating

An electric kettle is used to heat some water. When the kettle is on, energy is transferred

.... to the thermal energy store of the kettle's heating element.

The energy is then transferred .... to the water.

The energy is transferred to the water's .... energy store.

[Total 3 marks]

---

2 A block of aluminium is heated. The total amount of energy transferred to the block is 9000 J. The mass of the block is 200 g. *(Grade 4-5)*

2.1 Calculate the change in temperature of the block of aluminium when it is been heated.
The specific heat capacity of aluminium is 900 J/kg°C.
Use an equation from the Equations List.

Change in temperature = ... °C

[3]

2.2 Copper has a lower specific heat capacity than aluminium.
A 200 g block of copper is heated so its temperature changes by the same amount as
the aluminium. Use the correct phrase from the box below to complete the sentence.

more than	less than	the same as

The amount of energy needed to heat the copper block is ....

the amount of energy needed to heat the aluminium block.

[1]

[Total 4 marks]

Topic P1 — Energy

Investigating Specific Heat Capacity

1   A student is investigating the specific heat capacities of three liquids. She uses the apparatus shown in **Figure 1**.

Grade 3-4

She places 60 g of a liquid into a 100 ml flask. She measures the initial temperature of the liquid. 3000 J of energy is supplied to the liquid using an immersion heater. She then measures the final temperature and calculates the temperature change. She repeats this method for each liquid.

Figure 1

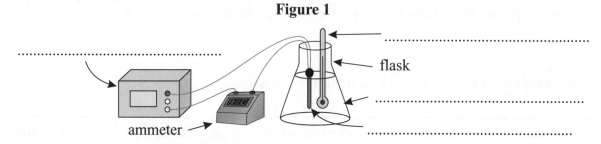

flask

ammeter

1.1 Use the phrases from the box to label the diagram in **Figure 1**.

| thermometer | liquid | power supply | immersion heater |

[3]

The student records her results, which are shown in **Table 1**.

Table 1

Liquid	Temperature change (°C)
A	12
B	23
C	25

1.2 Use the results in **Table 1** to list the liquids in order of increasing specific heat capacity.

Lowest specific heat capacity   ....

....

Highest specific heat capacity   ....

[1]

1.3 Which of the following would improve the accuracy of the experiment?
Tick **one** box.

Putting insulation around the flask. ☐

Using a more powerful power supply. ☐

Testing more liquids. ☐

[1]

[Total 5 marks]

Exam Practice Tip

You may be asked about experiments you've never seen before in an exam, but don't panic. Take your time to read the experiment carefully. Work out what's going on before attempting any questions to get full marks.

Power

Choose from the words on the left to fill in the blanks in the sentences on the right. You do not need to use all of the words.

joules
work done
total
watts
energy lost
rate of

Power is the .... energy transfer or

.... It is measured in ....

1 Two lamps, A and B, are turned on for 1 minute. Lamp A is more powerful than lamp B. Choose the correct letter below to complete the sentence.

A transfer less energy
B transfer more energy
C transfer the same amount of energy

Lamp A will .... over 1 minute than lamp B.

[Total 1 mark]

2 A student heats a beaker of water using an immersion heater. The immersion heater has a power of 35 W.

2.1 Calculate the work done by the immersion heater when it is operated for 600 s. Use the equation:

$$\text{power} = \frac{\text{work done}}{\text{time}}$$

Work done = ... J
[3]

2.2 The student then uses the immersion heater to heat a second beaker of water. The heater transferred 16 800 J of energy to the system. Calculate the time that the heater was on for.

Time = ... s
[4]

[Total 7 marks]

Exam Practice Tip

For really big powers, you might see the unit kW, which stands for kilowatt. Don't let this put you off though, you just need to remember that 1000 W = 1 kW. You might see this in a few other units too, for example 1000 m = 1 km.

Reducing Unwanted Energy Transfers

1 **Figure 1** shows a well.
The handle is turned, which rotates the axle.
The rope attached to the bucket
wraps around the axle.
This raises the bucket in the well.

Grade 3-4

Figure 1

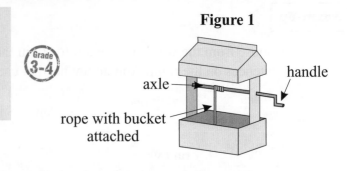

axle

handle

rope with bucket
attached

Use the correct words from the box
below to complete the sentence.

axle	more	less	always	lubricating
bucket		insulating	sometimes	

Energy is .... wasted when the handle is turned. The bucket rises faster

when .... energy is wasted. The speed at which the bucket rises will be

increased by .... the ....

[Total 4 marks]

2 A builder is building an energy-efficient house.

Grade 4-5

She has four types of brick to choose from to make the house walls.
Table 1 shows the thermal conductivity and thickness of each type of brick.

Table 1

Type	Thermal conductivity	Brick thickness (cm)
A	High	10
B	High	15
C	Low	10
D	Low	15

Based on the information in **Table 1**, state which type of brick she should use.
Explain your answer.

....

....

....

[Total 3 marks]

3 A student is charging her mobile phone.
She notices that the phone starts to heat up.
Explain why the phone starts to heat up.

Grade 4-5

....

....

[Total 2 marks]

Topic P1 — Energy

Efficiency

1 All appliances have an efficiency. (Grade 1-3)

1.1 Which of the following statements is true?
Tick **one** box.

Some modern appliances are 100% efficient. ☐

The more energy wasted by a device, the more efficient it is. ☐

Whenever energy is transferred, some energy is wasted. ☐

[1]

1.2 Choose the correct letter below to complete the sentence.
- **A** Decreasing the energy transferred to a device
- **B** Increasing the efficiency of a device
- **C** Decreasing the efficiency of a device

.... increases the amount of energy the device transfers to useful energy stores.

[1]

1.3 A toaster has an efficiency of 68%. A kettle has an efficiency of 0.75.
State whether the toaster or the kettle is more efficient.

....

[1]

[Total 3 marks]

2 To fully charge a mobile phone battery, 20 000 J must be transferred to it.
The battery transfers 16 000 J of this energy usefully until it needs to be charged again. (Grade 4-5)

Which calculation can be used to find the efficiency of the battery as a percentage? Tick **one** box.

(20 000 ÷ 16 000) ÷ 100 ☐

(20 000 ÷ 16 000) × 100 ☐

(16 000 ÷ 20 000) × 100 ☐

(16 000 ÷ 20 000) ÷ 100 ☐

[Total 1 mark]

3 An electric motor has a useful power output of 57 W and an efficiency of 75%. (Grade 4-5)

3.1 Write down the equation that links efficiency, useful power output and total power input.

....

[1]

3.2 Calculate the total power input for the motor.

Total power input = ... W

[3]

[Total 4 marks]

☹ ☐   ☺ ☐   ☺ ☐

Energy Resources and Their Uses

Energy resources are either renewable or non-renewable.
Write the energy resources below in the correct column of the table.

bio-fuel   oil

coal

hydro-electricity

solar

wind

nuclear fuel

tidal   geothermal

wave power   gas

Renewable	Non-renewable

1 Petrol or diesel is used to power most cars. They are both made from a fossil fuel. **Grade 1-3**

1.1 Name the **three** fossil fuels.

1. ....

2. ....

3. ....

[3]

1.2 Give **two** other everyday uses for fossil fuels.

1. ....

2. ....

[2]

1.3 Which of the following energy resources can be used to directly power some modern cars?
Tick **one** box.

Nuclear fuel ☐

Geothermal power ☐

Bio-fuel ☐

Hydro-electricity ☐

[1]

[Total 6 marks]

2 Describe the difference between renewable and non-renewable energy resources. **Grade 3-4**

....

....

....

[Total 2 marks]

Topic P1 — Energy

Wind, Solar and Geothermal

1 Wind turbines use wind power to generate electricity. Grade 3-4

1.1 Give **one** advantage and **one** disadvantage of using wind turbines to generate electricity.

Advantage: ....

....

Disadvantage: ....

....

[2]

1.2 Geothermal power uses hot rocks under the Earth's surface to generate electricity.
Give **one** advantage of using geothermal power to generate electricity.

....

....

[1]

[Total 3 marks]

2* A university wants to reduce their energy bills.
They want to build either a single wind turbine nearby, Grade 4-5
or install solar panels on top of their buildings.

The average wind speed for the university the previous year is shown in **Table 1**.
The average number of hours of sunlight per day is also given.

Table 1

	Average wind speed (m/s)	Average number of hours of daylight
October-March	8.0	9
April-September	4.3	15

The university decides to install both a wind turbine and solar panels.
Use the information in **Table 1** to suggest why.

....

....

....

....

....

....

....

....

[Total 4 marks]

Hydro-electricity, Waves and Tides

1 Wave-powered turbines are used to generate electricity. *Grade 1-3*

1.1 Which of the following statements about wave-powered turbines are true?
Tick **two** boxes.

They generate electricity all the time. ☐

They rely on light from the Sun to produce electricity. ☐

They must be placed near the coast. ☐

They produce pollution when generating electricity. ☐

They can disturb the habitats of animals. ☐

[2]

1.2 Hydro-electric power plants also use water to generate electricity.
Give **one** disadvantage of generating electricity from wave-powered turbines
compared to generating electricity from hydro-electric power plants.

....

[1]

[Total 3 marks]

2* An energy provider wants to build a new power plant.
They want to build either a hydro-electric power plant or a tidal barrage. *Grade 4-5*

Compare the reliability and the impact on the environment for generating
electricity from hydro-electric power plants and tidal barrages.

....

....

....

....

....

....

....

....

....

....

[Total 4 marks]

Exam Practice Tip

If you're asked to compare two energy resources, then make sure you are <u>comparing</u>. For example, if you were asked to compare the advantages and disadvantages of two resources, it's no good just listing the advantages and disadvantages of each. You need to talk about the advantages and disadvantages of each energy resource in relation to the other.

Topic P1 — Energy

Bio-fuels and Non-renewables

Put a ring around any statements that are **true** for nuclear power.

The waste produced is
difficult to dispose of.

It is a non-renewable
energy resource.

Nuclear power plants must
be built near the coast.

There is always a risk of
oil spills when using it to
generate electricity.

The radiation produced
when using nuclear power
is dangerous to humans.

1 Complete **Table 1** to show to show whether each statement applies
to bio-fuels, fossil fuels, or both. Tick **one** box in each row.

Table 1

	Bio-fuels	Fossil fuels	Both
They release carbon dioxide when they are burnt.			
They are a renewable energy resource.			
They are slowly running out.			

[Total 3 marks]

2* Describe the advantages and disadvantages of using fossil fuels to generate electricity.

....

....

....

....

....

....

....

....

....

....

....

....

[Total 6 marks]

Trends in Energy Resource Use

1 **Figure 1** shows the energy resources used to generate electricity in a country.

Figure 1

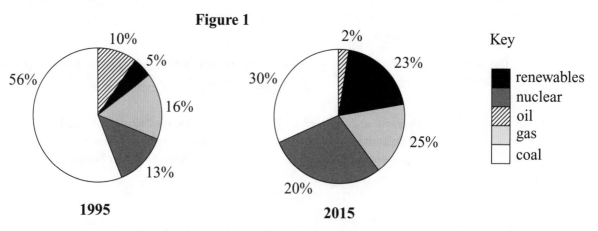

1.1 Determine what percentage of the country's electricity was generated by fossil fuels in 1995.

..........................%

[2]

1.2 Suggest **one** trend you can determine from the pie charts in **Figure 1**.

....

[1]

[Total 3 marks]

2 In the UK, the use of renewable energy resources is increasing. Some people say it is not increasing at a fast enough rate.

2.1 Suggest **one** reason for this increase in the use of renewable energy resources.

....

....

[2]

2.2* Suggest and explain the factors that may affect the rate at which we decrease our use of fossil fuels and increase our use of renewable energy resources.

....

....

....

....

....

....

....

[4]

[Total 6 marks]

Current and Circuit Symbols

Draw lines to match each circuit symbol to its correct name.

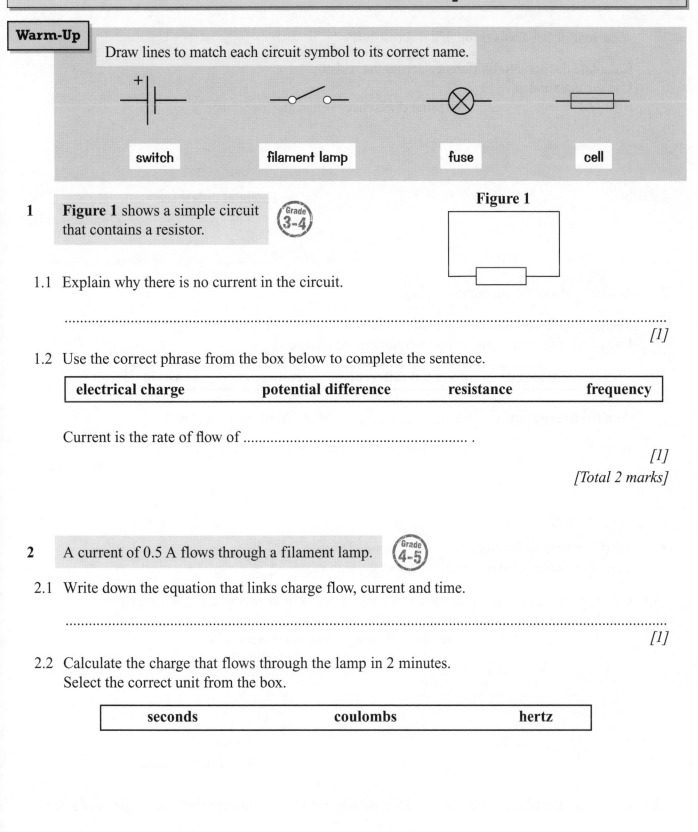

switch   filament lamp   fuse   cell

1 **Figure 1** shows a simple circuit that contains a resistor. (Grade 3-4)

Figure 1

1.1 Explain why there is no current in the circuit.

....

[1]

1.2 Use the correct phrase from the box below to complete the sentence.

electrical charge	potential difference	resistance	frequency

Current is the rate of flow of ....

[1]

[Total 2 marks]

2 A current of 0.5 A flows through a filament lamp. (Grade 4-5)

2.1 Write down the equation that links charge flow, current and time.

....

[1]

2.2 Calculate the charge that flows through the lamp in 2 minutes.
Select the correct unit from the box.

seconds	coulombs	hertz

Charge = ... Unit = ...

[4]

[Total 5 marks]

Exam Practice Tip

Make sure you learn the different circuit symbols. You'll need to be able to recognise them if they crop up in the exam.

Resistance and V = IR

1 A current of 3 A flows through a 6 Ω resistor. *(Grade 1-3)*

Calculate the potential difference across the resistor.
Use the equation:

$$\text{potential difference} = \text{current} \times \text{resistance}$$

Potential difference = ...V

[Total 2 marks]

2 A wire is an ohmic conductor. *(Grade 3-4)*

The passage below describes ohmic conductors.
Use phrases from the box below to complete the passage.

changed	potential difference	resistance	constant

At a fixed temperature, the .... of an ohmic conductor will

remain .... as the current through it is ....

[Total 3 marks]

3 When a potential difference of 25 V is applied across a filament lamp, a current of 3.0 A flows through it. *(Grade 4-5)*

3.1 Calculate the resistance of the filament lamp. Give your answer to 2 significant figures.
Use the equation:

$$\text{potential difference} = \text{current} \times \text{resistance}$$

Resistance = ... Ω

[3]

3.2 Over time, the filament gets hotter. Explain why the current through the lamp begins to decrease.

....

....

....

[2]

[Total 5 marks]

Investigating Resistance

1 A student investigated how the resistance of a piece of wire depends on its length. The circuit she used is shown in **Figure 1**. Her results are displayed in **Table 1**.

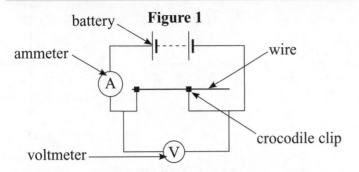

Figure 1

battery, ammeter, wire, crocodile clip, voltmeter

Table 1

Length / cm	Resistance / Ω
10	0.6
20	1.2
30	1.8
40	2.4
50	3.0

1.1 Complete the description of how the student used the results from her investigation in **Table 1** to calculate the resistance of each wire length. Use phrases from the box below to complete the sentence.

divided	ammeter	multiplied	power supply

The reading on the voltmeter was .... by the reading on the ....

[2]

1.2 Complete the graph in **Figure 2**, by plotting the remaining data points from **Table 1**. Draw a line of best fit on the graph.

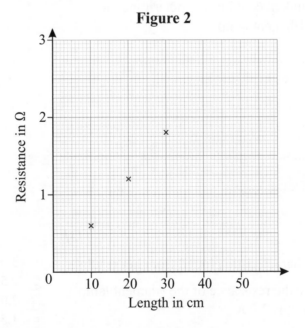

Figure 2

Resistance in Ω

Length in cm

[3]

1.3 What does the graph in **Figure 2** show? Tick **one** box.

Resistance is directly proportional to length. ☐

There is no relationship between resistance and length. ☐

Resistance is inversely proportional to length. ☐

Resistance increases with length up to a point, and then starts decreasing. ☐

[1]

[Total 6 marks]

I-V Characteristics

1　Electrical components can be linear or non-linear.

1.1　Which of the graphs below, **A**, **B**, **C** or **D**, is an *I-V* characteristic of a linear component?

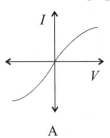 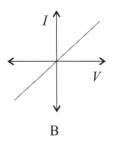 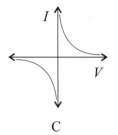 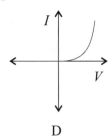

　　　A　　　　　　　　　　B　　　　　　　　　　C　　　　　　　　　　D

Your answer = ...
[1]

1.2　Give **one** example of a linear component.

....
[1]

[Total 2 marks]

2　A student is investigating the *I-V* characteristic of a filament lamp. She uses the circuit shown in **Figure 1**.

Figure 1

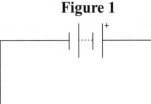

2.1　Describe a method the student could use to determine the *I-V* characteristic of the filament lamp.

....

....

....

....

....

....
[3]

2.2　**Figure 2** shows the *I-V* characteristic plotted from her results.

Using **Figure 2**, calculate the resistance of the filament lamp when the current through it is 2.0 A.

Figure 2

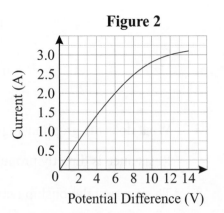

Resistance = ...Ω
[4]

[Total 7 marks]

Topic P2 — Electricity

Circuit Devices

1 A thermistor is a special kind of resistor.

Which of the graphs below shows how the resistance of a thermistor changes with temperature?
Tick **one** box.

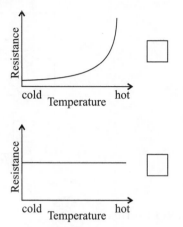

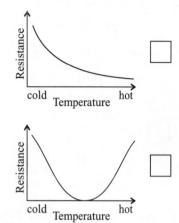

[Total 1 mark]

2 A student wants to measure the resistance of a light dependent resistor (LDR).

2.1 Draw the circuit diagram of a circuit that the student could use to measure
the resistance of an LDR. Use the circuit symbols shown in **Table 1**.

Table 1

battery	voltmeter	ammeter	LDR
+ —‖⋯‖⊢	—(V)—	—(A)—	LDR symbol

[2]

2.2 The resistance of an LDR depends on its surroundings.
State what happens to the resistance of an LDR as the surrounding light intensity increases.

....

[1]

2.3 Give **one** example of a device that uses a light dependent resistor.

....

[1]

[Total 4 marks]

Topic P2 — Electricity

Series Circuits

1 **Figure 1** shows three circuits. **One** of the circuits has **all** of its components connected in series. Tick the box below this circuit.

Grade 1-3

Figure 1

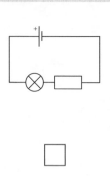
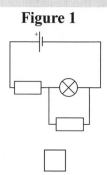
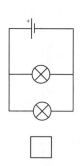

☐   ☐   ☐

[Total 1 mark]

2 **Figure 2** shows a circuit containing two resistors connected in series.

Grade 4-5

2.1 What is the total resistance of the circuit? Tick **one** box.

Figure 2

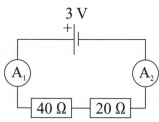

10 Ω   ☐

30 Ω   ☐

20 Ω   ☐

60 Ω   ☐

[1]

2.2 The reading on ammeter A_1 in **Figure 2** is 0.05 A.
Write down the reading on ammeter A_2.

Current = ... A
[1]

2.3 A third resistor is added in series to the circuit shown in **Figure 2**.
The potential difference across the 40 Ω resistor is 1.2 V.
The potential difference across the 20 Ω is 0.6 V.
Calculate the potential difference across the third resistor.

Potential difference = ... V
[2]

[Total 4 marks]

Exam Practice Tip

Ammeters and voltmeters have to be connected in a certain way, no matter what type of circuit you are making.
A voltmeter must always be connected in parallel with what you're measuring the potential difference across.
But the circuit will still count as a series circuit if everything else is connected around one loop of wire.

Parallel Circuits

In the circuit diagram on the right, which filament lamp is connected in parallel with the resistor? Tick **one** box.

A ☐

B ☐

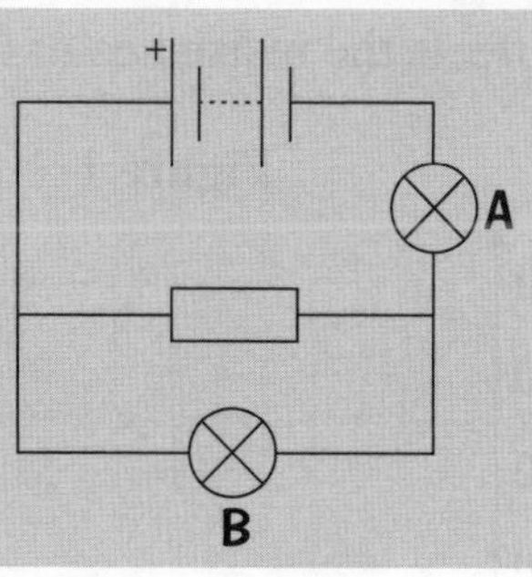

1   **Figure 1** shows a parallel circuit containing two identical resistors, R₁ and R₂.   (Grade 4-5)

1.1   The current through R₁ in **Figure 1** is 3 A.
The current through R₂ in **Figure 1** is 3 A.
What is the reading on the ammeter in **Figure 1**?
Tick **one** box.

3 A   ☐

1 A   ☐

0 A   ☐

6 A   ☐

[1]

Figure 1

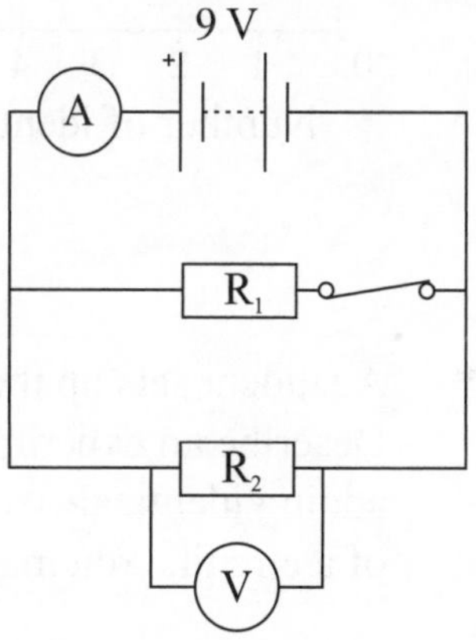

9 V

1.2   What is the reading on the voltmeter in **Figure 1**?
Tick **one** box.

3 V   ☐

0 V   ☐

9 V   ☐

1 V   ☐

[1]

Figure 2

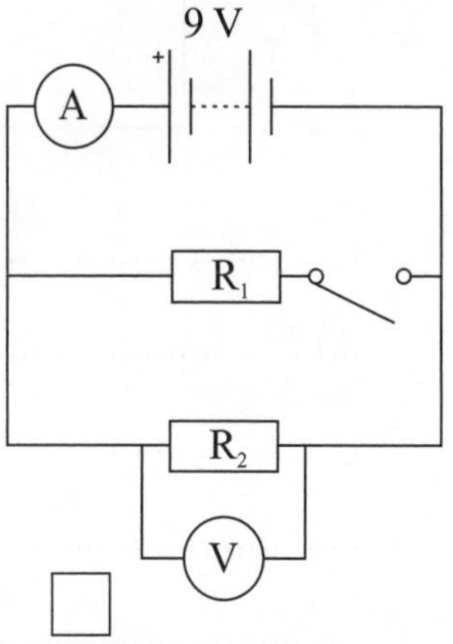

9 V

1.3   The switch is opened, as shown in **Figure 2**.
Which of the following statements about the
circuits in **Figure 1** and **Figure 2** is **true**?
Tick **one** box.

The total resistance of the circuit in **Figure 1** is larger than in **Figure 2**.   ☐

The total resistance of the circuit in **Figure 1** is smaller than in **Figure 2**.   ☐

The total resistance of the circuit in **Figure 1** is the same as in **Figure 2**.   ☐

[1]

[Total 3 marks]

Investigating Circuits

1 A student investigates how adding identical fixed resistors in series affects the resistance of the circuit. **Figure 1** shows his results.

Figure 1

The result for four resistors is anomalous.

1.1 Draw a line of best fit for the student's data on **Figure 1**.
[1]

1.2 Use your line of best fit to predict the correct resistance for the anomalous result.

Resistance = ... Ω
[1]

[Total 2 marks]

2* A student sets up the basic circuit shown in **Figure 2**.
Describe an experiment the student could do to investigate how adding identical fixed resistors in parallel affects the overall resistance of a circuit. You may draw a circuit diagram as part of your answer.

Figure 2

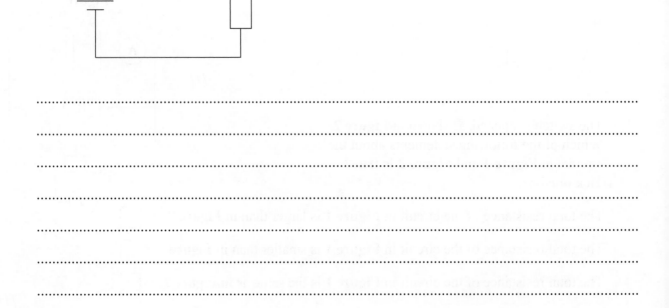

....

....

....

....

....

....

....

....

[Total 6 marks]

Electricity in the Home

Choose from the words below to complete the sentences about mains electricity in the UK.

| alternating | 50 | 0 | 230 | direct |

Mains electricity is a supply of .... current.

It is at .... V and has a frequency of .... Hz.

---

1 Most electrical appliances have an electrical cable containing a live wire, a neutral wire, and an earth wire.

Grade 1-3

1.1 Name this type of cable.

....

[1]

1.2 Each wire is coated in plastic insulation.
Draw **one** line from each wire to the colour of its insulation.

Wire

| neutral |
| earth |
| live |

Colour of insulation

| green and yellow |
| brown |
| blue |

[2]

1.3 The earth wire is a safety wire used in appliances that have metal cases.
Use words from the box below to complete the passage.

| current | live | resistance | neutral | frequency | earth |

When an appliance is working normally, ... flows to the appliance

through the .... wire and the .... wire.

The .... wire will only carry current if there is a fault.

[4]

1.4 State what could happen if a person touched an exposed live wire.

....

[1]

[Total 8 marks]

Exam Practice Tip

Learning the potential difference and frequency of the UK mains supply could get you some easy marks in the exam.

Power of Electrical Appliances

1   The power source for a remote-controlled car is a battery.   **(Grade 1-3)**

Which of the following is the main energy transfer from the battery to the toy car?
Tick **one** box.

By heating to the electrostatic energy store of the car's motor. ☐

Electrically to the nuclear energy store of the car's motor. ☐

Electrically to the kinetic energy store of the car's motor. ☐

Mechanically to the elastic potential energy store of the car's motor. ☐

[Total 1 mark]

2   Use the correct phrases from the box to complete the sentences below.   **(Grade 3-4)**

charges	power	in total	per second	potential difference	safety

The .... of an appliance is the energy transferred ....

Energy is transferred because the .... do work against the appliance's resistance.

[Total 3 marks]

3   A student uses a 700 W microwave to heat a bowl of soup.   **(Grade 4-5)**

3.1   Write down the equation that links energy transferred, power and time.

....

[1]

3.2   The microwave transfers 140 000 J to heat the bowl of soup.
Calculate the time it takes to heat the soup.

Time taken = ... s

[3]

3.3   The student buys a new microwave. The new microwave has a power rating of 900 W.
Explain why the 900 W microwave heats the soup faster than the 700 W microwave.

....

....

....

[2]

[Total 6 marks]

Topic P2 — Electricity

More on Power

1   **Figure 1** shows a circuit. The reading on the voltmeter is 6 V.

Figure 1

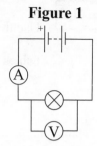

1.1   The reading on the ammeter in **Figure 1** is 2 A.
Calculate the power of the filament lamp. Use the equation:

$$\text{power} = \text{potential difference} \times \text{current}$$

Power = ... W

[2]

1.2   Write down the equation that links energy transferred, charge flow and potential difference.

....

[1]

1.3   Calculate the energy transferred to the lamp when 4 C of charge passes through it.

Energy transferred = ... J

[2]

[Total 5 marks]

2   A motor with a power of 1.5 kW has a resistance of 70 Ω.

The equation that links power, current and resistance is:

$$\text{power} = (\text{current})^2 \times \text{resistance}$$

Which calculation gives the current flowing through the motor in amps?
Tick **one** box.

$\text{current} = \sqrt{\dfrac{1500}{70}}$ ☐

$\text{current} = \sqrt{\dfrac{1.5}{140}}$ ☐

$\text{current} = \sqrt{\dfrac{70}{1500}}$ ☐

$\text{current} = 1500 \times 70$ ☐

[Total 1 mark]

Exam Practice Tip

There's a lot of equations to do with power, but try not to panic about them. If you're not sure which one to use, look at the values you've been given, or have already calculated in the question. Then use the equation which involves those.

Topic P2 — Electricity

172

The National Grid

Use the words given below to label the diagram.

cables   power station   step-up transformer   step-down transformer

pylons

consumers

1   Which of the following correctly describes the effect of a step-down transformer? Tick **one** box.   *Grade 3-4*

It increases the output current and the output potential difference. ☐

It increases the output current and decreases the output potential difference. ☐

It decreases the output current and increases the output potential difference. ☐

It decreases the output current and the output potential difference. ☐

[Total 1 mark]

2   The national grid has to transfer a lot of energy very quickly, so it transmits electricity at a very high power. To transmit electricity at a high power, the electricity must either have a high current or a high potential difference.   *Grade 4-5*

Explain why the national grid is an efficient way of transferring energy.

....

....

....

....

....

....

[Total 4 marks]

Exam Practice Tip

You don't need to understand how transformers work, just what they're used for and the difference between the two types.

Topic P2 — Electricity

The Particle Model and Motion in Gases

The images below show the particles for a substance in three states.
Label each image to show whether the substance is a solid, a liquid or a gas.

....

1 A sample of ice is heated so that it melts.
The water is then heated until it evaporates.
The water has changed from a solid to a liquid to a gas.

Grade 1-3

What is the difference between the water in these states?
Tick **one** box.

The size of the water particles.   ☐

The energy stored by the particles.   ☐

What the water particles are made of.   ☐

[Total 1 mark]

2 A tyre is pumped up to its maximum volume.   *Grade 3-4*

How will the tyre pressure be different on a hot day compared to a cold day?
Tick **one** box.

The tyre pressure on a hot day will be higher than the tyre pressure on a cold day.   ☐

The tyre pressure on a hot day will be lower than the tyre pressure on a cold day.   ☐

The tyre pressure on a hot day will be the same as the tyre pressure on a cold day.   ☐

[Total 1 mark]

3 As a gas is cooled, its temperature decreases. Explain what happens
to the energy and speed of the particles in the gas when it is cooled.   *Grade 4-5*

....

....

....

[Total 2 marks]

Density of Materials

1 An irregularly shaped stone has an unknown volume. **Grade 1-3**

What equipment can be used for finding the volume of the stone?
Tick **one** box.

a thermometer ☐

a eureka can ☐

a mass balance ☐

a ruler ☐

a stopwatch ☐

[Total 1 mark]

2 A 1.5 m³ block of tungsten has a mass of 28 875 kg. **Grade 4-5**

2.1 Write down the equation that links density, mass and volume.

....

[1]

2.2 Calculate the density of tungsten. Give your answer to 2 significant figures.

Density = ... kg/m³
[2]

[Total 3 marks]

PRACTICAL

3* A student has a mass balance, a measuring cylinder and some acid (a liquid). **Grade 4-5**
She wants to use the equipment to find the density of the acid.

Describe an experiment the student could do to calculate the density of the acid.

....

....

....

....

....

[Total 4 marks]

Exam Practice Tip

You might be asked to explain an experiment that is used to find the density of an object. Make sure you know the different equipment you would need for finding the density of a solid or a liquid. You should be able to explain how the equipment is used. You also need to be able to explain how the results are used to calculate the density.

Topic P3 — Particle Model of Matter

Internal Energy and Changes of State

1 Use words from the box below to complete the passage.

mass	increases	temperature	density	decreases

When a system is heated, the internal energy of the system .... This either

increases the .... of the system or causes a change of state. During a change

of state the temperature and the .... of the substance remain constant.

[Total 3 marks]

2 Heating or cooling a substance can lead to a change of state.

2.1 Name the following changes of state:

Gas to liquid: ....

Liquid to gas: ....

[2]

2.2 A change of state is a physical change. Define the term 'physical change'.

....

....

[1]

[Total 3 marks]

3 A student fills a test tube with 30 g of water. He then heats the water.
Heating the water increases the internal energy of the water.

3.1 Define the term 'internal energy'.

....

....

[1]

3.2 The student continues to heat the water so that it starts to boil.
When the water boils it becomes water vapour.
He collects all of the water vapour produced.
He stops boiling the water. The mass of the water in the test tube is now 20 g.

State the mass of the water vapour the student collected.
Explain your answer.

....

....

....

[2]

[Total 3 marks]

Topic P3 — Particle Model of Matter

Specific Latent Heat

1 A sealed box containing a solid substance is heated.
Figure 1 shows a graph of temperature against time as the substance is heated.

Figure 1

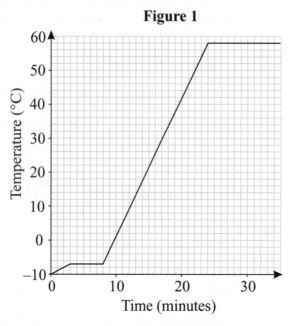

Time (minutes)

1.1 Draw straight lines to match the time period on the left
to what is happening with the substance on the right.

Time period

Between 3 and 8 minutes.

Between 24 and 35 minutes.

Between 8 and 24 minutes.

Substance

Substance is a liquid being heated.

Substance is melting.

Substance is boiling.

Substance is a solid being heated.

Substance is freezing.

[3]

1.2 The substance has a mass of 0.50 kg.
34 000 J of energy is transferred to the substance to completely melt it.
The temperature of the substance does not change during this time.

Calculate the specific latent heat of fusion of the substance.
Use an equation from the Equations List.

Specific latent heat = ... J/kg

[3]

[Total 6 marks]

The Current Model of the Atom

Warm-Up

What is the typical radius of an atom?

☐ 1×10^{-10} m   ☐ 1×10^{10} m   ☐ 1×10^{-20} m   ☐ 1×10^{-15} m

1 Scientists currently agree that a nuclear model is the best description of the atom we have. **Grade 1-3**

1.1 The passage below describes the nuclear model of the atom.
Use words from the box below to complete the passage.

| electrons | neutrons | size | protons | positively | mass | negatively |

An atom is made of a ....-charged nucleus, surrounded by ....

The nucleus contains .... and ....

The nucleus makes up most of the .... of the atom.

[5]

1.2 How many times smaller is the radius of the nucleus compared to the radius of the atom?
Tick **one** box.

10 000   ☐

100 000   ☐

10   ☐

[1]

[Total 6 marks]

2 Niels Bohr discovered that electrons within an atom can only exist in defined energy levels. **Grade 4-5**

2.1 Atoms can emit and absorb electromagnetic radiation.
Describe how this affects the positions of electrons in the atom.

....

....

....

....

[3]

2.2 An atom loses an electron. Is the new particle positively, negatively or neutrally charged?
Explain why.

....

....

[2]

[Total 5 marks]

 ☐   ☐   ☐

Isotopes and Nuclear Radiation

1 Some isotopes are unstable. They emit nuclear radiation. **Grade 3-4**

1.1 Draw **one** line from each term to the correct definition.

Term

Isotopes

Gamma

Alpha particles

Definition

Atoms with the same number of protons but different numbers of neutrons.

Particles made up of two neutrons and two protons.

Nuclear radiation made up of electromagnetic waves.

[2]

1.2 An unstable isotope decays. It releases a high-speed electron from its nucleus. Name this type of radioactive decay.

....

[1]

[Total 3 marks]

2 One isotope of sodium is $^{23}_{11}$Na. **Grade 4-5**

2.1 Write down the mass number of this isotope.

....

[1]

2.2 Calculate the number of neutrons in the sodium nucleus.

Number of neutrons = ...

[1]

2.3 Which of the following is another isotope of sodium? Tick **one** box.

$^{11}_{23}$Na ☐ $^{11}_{24}$Na ☐ $^{23}_{12}$Na ☐ $^{24}_{11}$Na ☐

[1]

[Total 3 marks]

3 Beta sources are used when making paper. Beta particles pass through the paper and the count-rate is measured. The paper is then made thicker or thinner depending on the count-rate measured. **Grade 4-5**

Explain why a source that emits alpha particles or gamma rays couldn't be used for this purpose.

....

....

....

[Total 2 marks]

Topic P4 — Atomic Structure

Nuclear Equations

Warm-Up

The nuclear equation below shows an atom releasing a gamma ray.
Complete the nuclear equation by filling in the missing number.

$$^{99}_{44}\text{Ru} \rightarrow ^{99}_{44}\text{Ru} + ^{0}_{.....}\gamma$$

1 A strontium-90 nucleus decays by beta emission to form yttrium-90.

$$^{90}_{38}\text{Sr} \rightarrow ^{90}_{39}\text{Y} + ^{0}_{-1}\text{e}$$

1.1 Describe how the mass number and atomic number of the nucleus change during the decay.

Mass number: ....

Atomic number: ....

[2]

1.2 How does the charge of the nucleus change after this decay? Tick **one** box.

It increases. ☐

It decreases. ☐

There is no change. ☐

[1]

[Total 3 marks]

2 A student writes down the following nuclear decay equation: (Grade 4-5)

$$^{226}_{88}\text{Ra} \rightarrow ^{a}_{b}\text{Rn} + ^{4}_{2}\text{X}$$

2.1 What particle is represented by **X** in the nuclear decay equation above?

....

[1]

2.2 Calculate the values of a and b.

a = ...

b = ...

[2]

2.3 The radon (Rn) isotope then undergoes an alpha decay to form an isotope of polonium (Po).
Write a balanced nuclear equation to show this.

....

[3]

[Total 6 marks]

Topic P4 — Atomic Structure

Half-life

1   The passage below describes terms relating to radioactive decay. Use words from the box below to complete the passage.

| activity | becquerels | half-life | radiation | watts |

The .... is the time taken for the number of nuclei of a radioactive

isotope in a sample to halve. The rate of decay of a radioactive isotope is called

its .... and it is measured in ....

[Total 3 marks]

2   The graph in **Figure 1** shows how the count-rate of a radioactive sample changes over time.

Figure 1

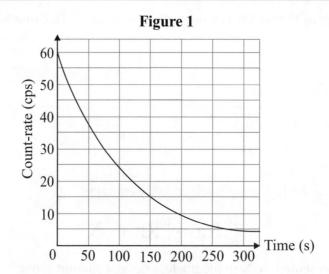

2.1   Using **Figure 1**, determine the half-life of the sample.

Half-life = ... s

[1]

2.2   At first, the sample contains approximately 800 undecayed nuclei.
Predict how many of these nuclei will have decayed after two half-lives.

Number of decayed nuclei = ...

[2]

[Total 3 marks]

Topic P4 — Atomic Structure

Irradiation and Contamination

1 Workers in a nuclear power station are at risk of being irradiated by nuclear radiation. Which of the following methods would reduce their risk of irradiation? Tick **one** box. *Grade 1-3*

Work behind barriers that absorb radiation. ☐

Keep fire extinguishers close by. ☐

Wear clean clothes. ☐

[Total 1 mark]

2 A scientist is looking at the safety plans to be used in her lab while using radioactive isotopes. She is worried about **contamination** and **irradiation**. *Grade 4-5*

2.1 Explain the difference between contamination and irradiation.

....

....

....

....

[2]

2.2 Give **two** ways the scientist can protect herself against **contamination** when handling radioactive isotopes.

1. ....

2. ....

[2]

[Total 4 marks]

3 Radium-226 is an alpha source. Radium-226 was used in clocks until the 1960s. *Grade 4-5*

Should a clockmaker be more worried about contamination or irradiation when working on clocks made before 1960? Explain your answer.

....

....

....

....

....

[Total 3 marks]

Exam Practice Tip

Make sure you learn the differences between irradiation and contamination and how to lower the risks of both. Remember, the dangers of irradiation or contamination depend on the type of radiation.

 ☐   ☐   ☐

Topic P4 — Atomic Structure

Contact and Non-Contact Forces

Each quantity below is either a scalar or a vector.
Write each word in the correct place in the table.

acceleration   time   temperature

mass   velocity   force

Scalar	Vector

1 Which of the following correctly describes a vector? Tick **one** box.

Vector quantities only have magnitude. ☐

Vector quantities have direction but not magnitude. ☐

Vector quantities have both magnitude and direction. ☐

[Total 1 mark]

2 A child is pulling a toy train along the floor using a piece of string.
State **one** contact force and **one** non-contact force that acts on the toy.

Contact force: ....

Non-contact force: ....

[Total 2 marks]

3 **Figure 1** shows two pairs of identical magnets. There is a force of repulsion between
Magnet A and Magnet B. There is a force of attraction between Magnet C and Magnet D.

Figure 1

Magnet A and Magnet B

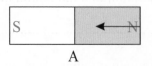   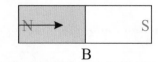

A   B

Magnet C and Magnet D

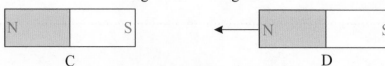

C   D

Complete the diagram in **Figure 1** by drawing an arrow that
represents the force Magnet D exerts on Magnet C.

[Total 2 marks]

Weight, Mass and Gravity

1 Draw **one** line from each property to the unit it is measured in. [Grade 1-3]

Property	Unit
mass	kilograms
weight	newtons

[Total 1 mark]

2 Which of the following correctly describes the relationship between mass and weight? Tick **one** box. [Grade 3-4]

Mass and weight are inversely proportional. ☐

Mass and weight are directly proportional. ☐

Mass and weight are the same thing. ☐

There is no relationship between mass and weight. ☐

[Total 1 mark]

3 Opportunity is a robot which is currently on the surface of the planet Mars. The total mass of Opportunity is 185 kg. [Grade 4-5]

3.1 Write down the equation that links weight, mass and gravitational field strength.

....

[1]

3.2 Calculate the weight of Opportunity when it was on the Earth.
(The gravitational field strength on the surface of Earth = 9.8 N/kg.)
Give your answer to 2 significant figures.

Weight = ... N

[2]

3.3 The weight of Opportunity on Mars is 703 N.
Calculate the gravitational field strength on the surface of Mars.

Gravitational Field Strength = ... N/kg

[3]

[Total 6 marks]

Exam Practice Tip

Outside of physics, people often use the term weight when they mean mass. Make sure you understand the difference. You measure mass on a balance, but weight is a force measured by a spring-balance (newtonmeter).

Resultant Forces and Work Done

1   **Figure 1** shows four runners who are running in windy weather.
    Tick the box under the runner who is experiencing the largest resultant force.

Figure 1

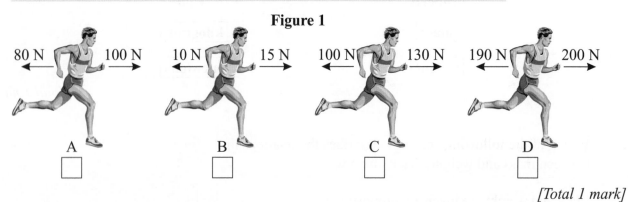

80 N ← → 100 N   10 N ← → 15 N   100 N ← → 130 N   190 N ← → 200 N

A ☐   B ☐   C ☐   D ☐

[Total 1 mark]

2   **Figure 2** shows two forces acting on a trolley.
    A force of 10 N acts to the left and 15 N acts to the right.

Figure 2

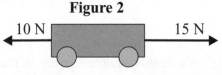

10 N ←   → 15 N

Calculate the resultant force on the trolley. Give its size and direction.

Size of resultant force = ... N

Direction = ...
[Total 2 marks]

3   A woman pulls a 20 kg suitcase along a 15 m corridor using a horizontal force of 50 N.

3.1 Calculate the work done by the woman. Use the equation:
                Work done = force × distance

Work done = ... Nm
[2]

3.2 Work is done against frictional forces acting on the wheels of the suitcase.
     Describe the effect this has on the temperature of wheels. Explain this in terms of energy transfer.

....

....
[2]
[Total 4 marks]

        ☐   ☐   ☐

Forces and Elasticity

1 A student hangs masses from a string. This causes the spring to stretch. **Grade 3-4**

  1.1 Two forces are being applied to the spring to make it stretch.
Explain why more than one force is needed to make the spring stretch.

....

....

[1]

  1.2 The student removes the masses. The spring returns to its original length and shape.
Name this type of deformation.

....

[1]

  1.3 The student adds more masses to the spring.
When the masses are removed, the spring doesn't return to its original shape.
Name this type of deformation.

....

[1]

[Total 3 marks]

2 A child sits on the toy horse in **Figure 1**. His feet don't touch the floor. **Grade 4-5**

Figure 1

The child exerts a force of 240 N on the horse.
The height of the toy horse decreases by 0.20 m.
Calculate the spring constant of the spring.
Use the equation:

force = spring constant × extension

Choose the correct unit from the box.

N/m	N/kg	kg m³

Spring constant = ... Unit = ...

[Total 4 marks]

Investigating Springs

PRACTICAL

1 A student investigated the relationship between the force exerted on, and the extension of, a spring. He hung different numbers of masses from the bottom of the spring. Each time he measured the extension of the spring with a ruler. His set up is shown in **Figure 1**.

Figure 1

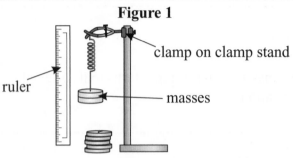

ruler

clamp on clamp stand

masses

Table 1	
Force (N)	Extension (cm)
0	0
1	3.0
2	6.0
3	9.0
4	12.0
5	16.5
6	24.5

Figure 2

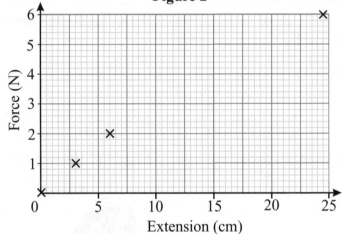

1.1 **Table 1** shows the results that the student obtained in his investigation. Complete the force-extension graph in **Figure 2** by plotting the **three** missing points from **Table 1** and drawing a line of best fit.

[3]

1.2 What name is given to the point on the graph where force and extension stop being directly proportional?

....

[1]

[Total 4 marks]

2 A spring is extended elastically by 8.0 cm. The spring constant of the spring is 25 N/m.

Calculate the work done on the spring. Use an equation from the Equations List.

Work done = ... J

[Total 3 marks]

Exam Practice Tip

You need to know the practical above really well — you could be asked about it in the exam. And make sure you draw graphs accurately with a sharp pencil. It'll really help if you need to use the graph to work something out.

Topic P5 — Forces

Distance, Displacement, Speed and Velocity

1   **Figure 1** shows the path taken by a football kicked by a child. When it is kicked at point A, the ball moves horizontally to the right until it hits a vertical wall at point B. The ball then bounces back horizontally to the left and comes to rest at point C.

Figure 1

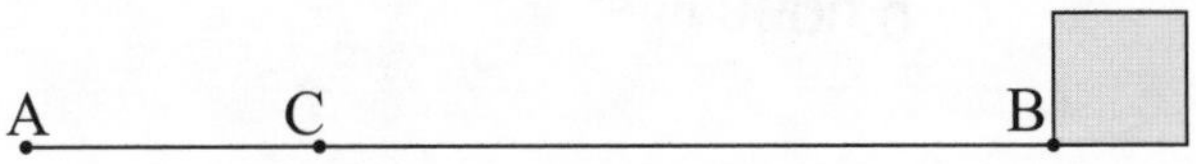

A   C   B   Scale 1 cm = 1 m

1.1 What is the total distance travelled by the ball as it moves from A to B?

Distance = ... m

[1]

1.2 Calculate the total distance travelled by the ball.

Distance = ... m

[1]

1.3 What is the magnitude of the displacement of the ball after it has come to rest?

Displacement = ... m

[1]

[Total 3 marks]

2   A man has just got a new job and wants to know how long it will take to get to work. His route to work is along a 6 km path.

2.1 What is the typical walking speed of a person?

Typical speed = ... m/s

[1]

2.2 Give **three** factors that can affect a person's walking speed.

1. ....

2. ....

3. ....

[3]

2.3 Write down the formula that links distance travelled, speed and time.

....

[1]

2.4 Estimate how long it would take the man to walk to work.

Time taken = ... s

[4]

[Total 9 marks]

Acceleration

Circle the value below that is the acceleration of an object falling freely on Earth.

9800 m/s^2 98 m/s^2 9.8 m/s^2

0.0098 m/s^2

1 An object is decelerating. Tick **one** box which describes its motion.

Moving with increasing velocity ☐
Moving with decreasing velocity ☐
Moving with a uniform velocity ☐
Stationary ☐

[Total 1 mark]

2 **Table 1** shows how the velocity of a car changes with time as it accelerates uniformly.

Table 1

Time (s)	0	1	2	3
Velocity (m/s)	0	4	8	12

2.1 Write down the formula that links acceleration, velocity and time.

....

[1]

2.2 Calculate the acceleration of the car.

Acceleration = ... m/s^2
[2]
[Total 3 marks]

3 A train is travelling at 18 m/s. It speeds up to 32 m/s over a distance of 350 m. Calculate the acceleration of the train over this distance. Use an equation from the Equations List.

Acceleration = ... m/s^2
[Total 3 marks]

Distance-Time Graphs

1 A boat is being rowed along a straight canal. Some students use a watch to time how long after setting off the boat passes markers spaced 100 metres apart. **Table 1** shows their results.

Table 1

Distance (m)	0	100	200	300	400	500
Time (s)	0	85	170	255	340	425

Figure 1

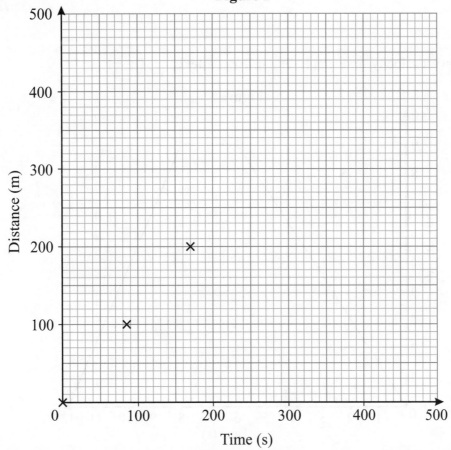

1.1 Complete the distance-time graph in **Figure 1** using the results in **Table 1**.

[3]

1.2 Using the graph in **Figure 1**, estimate how far the boat travelled in 300 s.

Distance = ... m

[1]

1.3 Using the graph in **Figure 1**, estimate how long it took the boat to travel 250 m.

Time = ... s

[1]

1.4 Describe the boat's speed during the first 500 m of its journey.

....

[1]

[Total 6 marks]

Topic P5 — Forces

Velocity-Time Graphs and Terminal Velocity

1 Any object falling for long enough reaches its terminal velocity.
Which statements correctly describe terminal velocity? Tick **two** boxes.

Terminal velocity is the minimum velocity an object can fall at. ☐

The resultant vertical force on an object falling at its terminal velocity is zero. ☐

The resultant vertical force on an object falling at its terminal velocity equals its weight. ☐

Terminal velocity is the maximum velocity an object can fall at. ☐

[Total 1 mark]

2 **Figure 1** shows a velocity-time graph for a roller coaster car.

Figure 1

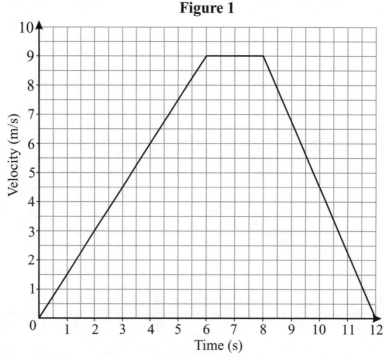

2.1 The car is accelerating between 0 s and 6 s.
Using the graph in **Figure 1**, calculate the acceleration for the ride between 0 s and 6 s.

Acceleration = ... m/s^2

[3]

2.2 Between what times is the car travelling at a constant speed?

....

[1]

[Total 4 marks]

Topic P5 — Forces

Newton's First and Second Laws

1 State Newton's First Law for a stationary object.

....

....

[Total 1 mark]

2 The passage below describes Newton's Second Law.
Use words from the box below to complete the passage.

area	weight	mass	driving	resistive	resultant

Newton's Second Law states that the acceleration of an object is directly

proportional to the .... force acting on the object.

Newton's Second Law also says that the acceleration is inversely proportional to the

.... of the object.

[Total 2 marks]

3 **Figure 1** shows an accelerating motorbike. It shows the resultant force acting on
the motorbike. The motorbike and rider have a combined mass of 400 kg.

Figure 1

2400 N

Calculate the acceleration of the motorbike. Use the equation:

Force = mass × acceleration

Choose the correct unit from the box.

N	kg	m/s^2

Acceleration = ... Unit = ...

[Total 4 marks]

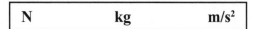

Topic P5 — Forces

Newton's Third Law

Which of the following is Newton's Third Law? Tick **one** box.

A resultant force is inversely proportional to the mass of an object. ☐

When two objects interact, they exert equal and opposite forces on each other. ☐

A resultant force of zero leads to an equilibrium situation. ☐

1   **Figure 1** shows skater A pushing on skater B with a force of 100 N. Using Newton's Third Law, what force does skater B exert on skater A? Tick **one** box.

Grade 1-3

Figure 1

50 N ☐

150 N ☐

200 N ☐

100 N ☐

[Total 1 mark]

2   **Figure 2** shows the forces acting on a gymnast balancing on two beams. The gymnast is in equilibrium.

Grade 4-5

Figure 2

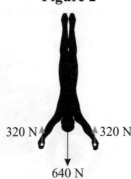

320 N↑   ↑320 N

↓
640 N

2.1 State the size of the force exerted by each of the gymnast's hands on the balance beams.

Force = ... N

[1]

2.2 State the size of the attractive force exerted on the Earth by the gymnast.

Force = ... N

[1]

[Total 2 marks]

Exam Practice Tip

If you're struggling to see what's going on in a question, try drawing a quick diagram. Make sure it shows all the forces mentioned in the question. Then look at each force one at a time to work out what effect it's having.

☹ ☐   🙂 ☐   😀 ☐

Investigating Motion

1 **Figure 1** shows the equipment used by a student to investigate how changing the force on a trolley changes its acceleration. The trolley is on a frictionless, flat surface.

Figure 1

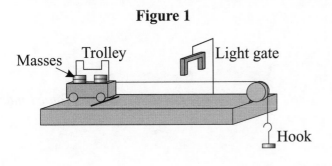

Masses Trolley Light gate Hook

Figure 2

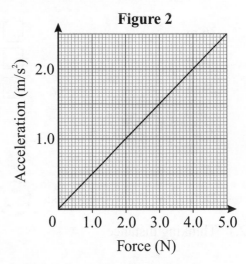

The student changes the force on the trolley by moving a mass from the trolley to the hook. The acceleration for different forces is recorded.
Figure 2 is a graph of acceleration against force for the trolley.

1.1 For this experiment, what is the mass being accelerated? Tick **one** box.

The mass of the hook. ☐

The mass of the hook and the trolley. ☐

The mass of the trolley. ☐

[1]

1.2 Give **one** conclusion that can be made from **Figure 2**.

....

....
[1]

1.3 Using **Figure 2**, calculate the mass being accelerated. Use the equation:
$$\text{Force} = \text{mass} \times \text{acceleration}$$

Mass = ... kg
[3]

1.4 The mass on the hook was kept the same. 50 g of mass was added to the trolley.
What effect will this have on the acceleration of the trolley?

....
[1]

[Total 6 marks]

Topic P5 — Forces

Stopping Distance and Thinking Distance

1 A car is travelling at 40 mph. The thinking distance of the driver is 12 m. The braking distance of the car is 24 m. Calculate the car's stopping distance when it is travelling at 40 mph. Tick **one** box.

36 m ☐

12 m ☐

24 m ☐

[Total 1 mark]

2 Define the following terms:

2.1 Thinking distance

....

[1]

2.2 Braking distance

....

[1]

[Total 2 marks]

3 Give **three** things that could affect a person's reaction time.

1. ....

2. ....

3. ....

[Total 3 marks]

4 Explain why a driver with a slower than average reaction time has an increased risk of being in an accident.

....

....

....

[Total 2 marks]

Braking Distance

Circle the factors below which affect the braking distance of a vehicle.

Drinking alcohol   Broken headlights   Snow on the road

Bald tyres   Drug use

Driver distractions

Ice on the road   Smooth road surface

1   A heavy vehicle travelling quickly can have a very large deceleration.
State **two** dangers of large decelerations.   Grade 1-3

1. ....

2. ....

[Total 2 marks]

2   When a vehicle's brakes are applied, friction between the wheels and brakes
causes work to be done. Explain how this affects the temperature of the brakes.   Grade 4-5
You should include a description of the energy transfers that occur.

....

....

....

....

[Total 2 marks]

3*   Explain the importance of car tyres that are in good condition when driving in the rain.   Grade 4-5
Explain the effect this will have on the stopping distance and the overall safety of the car.

....

....

....

....

....

....

....

....

[Total 4 marks]

Reaction Times

1 What is the typical reaction time for a person? Tick **one** box. (Grade 1-3)

☐ 1.3 – 1.8 s   ☐ 0.2 – 0.9 s   ☐ 0.01 – 0.02 s   ☐ 2.0 – 3.0 s

[Total 1 mark]

2 A teacher tests the reaction times of three of her students. (Grade 4-5)
She measures how far a ruler vertically falls before the student catches it.

2.1 Describe **one** other method that can be used to test people's reaction times.

....

....

[1]

2.2 **Table 1** shows the teacher's results.
The values in the table show the distance the ruler falls in cm during each attempt.
Complete the table by working out the average distance fallen by the ruler for each student.

Table 1

	Attempt 1	Attempt 2	Attempt 3	Average
Student A	7.0	7.1	6.9	....
Student B	8.4	8.2	8.3	....
Student C	6.5	7	6	6.5

[2]

2.3 Which student has the fastest average reaction time?

....

[1]

2.4 Suggest **two** ways the teacher could make the experiment a fair test.

1. ....

2. ....

[2]

2.5 The teacher then repeats the experiment. This time, she has a fourth student talk to the student
being tested. Suggest how you would expect this to affect the reaction times of the students.

....

[1]

[Total 7 marks]

Topic P5 — Forces

Transverse and Longitudinal Waves

Label the waves below with a T or an L to show whether
they are transverse waves (**T**) or longitudinal waves (**L**).

sound waves ......   ripples on water ......   light ......

1   **Figure 1** shows a displacement-distance graph of a wave.

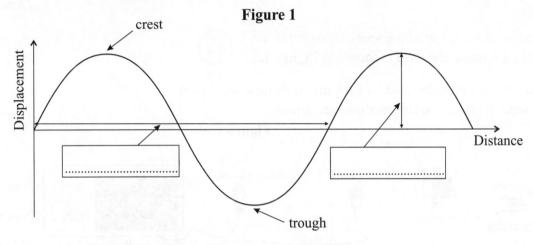

Figure 1

crest

trough

1.1   Use phrases from the box to complete the labels in **Figure 1**.

wavelength	period	rest position	amplitude

[2]

1.2   What is meant by the term 'frequency'?

....

[1]

1.3   Describe the difference between longitudinal waves and transverse waves.

....

....

....

[2]

[Total 5 marks]

2   A child throws a stone into a pond. The stone creates ripples
when it hits the water. These ripples spread across the pond.

The child thinks that a leaf floating on the pond will move to the edge of
the pond with the ripples. Explain whether or not she is correct.

....

....

....

[Total 2 marks]

Frequency, Period and Wave Speed

1 A wave has a period of 2 s.

Calculate the frequency of the wave. Use the equation:

$$\text{frequency} = 1 \div \text{period}$$

Frequency = ... Hz

[Total 2 marks]

2 A student investigated the speed of sound in air. The equipment she used is shown in **Figure 1**.

The sound waves detected by each microphone were shown as separate traces on the oscilloscope screen.

Figure 1

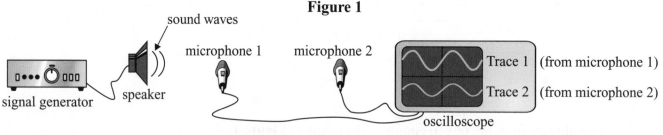

2.1 Her method is described below in steps **A** to **E**.
Steps **A** to **E** are not in the correct order.

A Measure the distance between the microphones. This is the wavelength.
B Stop moving microphone 2 when the traces line up, as shown in **Figure 1**.
C Use the measured distance and the frequency of the signal generator to find the wave speed.
D Begin with both microphones at an equal distance from the speaker.
E Keeping microphone 1 fixed, slowly move microphone 2 away from the speaker, causing trace 2 to move.

In the spaces below, write down the correct order of steps.
The first one has been done for you.

D $\longrightarrow$ .... $\longrightarrow$ .... $\longrightarrow$ .... $\longrightarrow$ ....

....

[3]

2.2 Write down the equation that relates wave speed, frequency and wavelength.

....

[1]

2.3 The signal generator is set to 50.0 Hz. The wavelength of the sound waves is measured to be 6.80 m. Calculate the speed of the sound waves.

Wave speed = ... m/s

[2]

[Total 6 marks]

Investigating Waves

1 A student produces a wave on a string using a vibration generator. A snapshot of the wave on the string is shown in **Figure 1**.

Figure 1

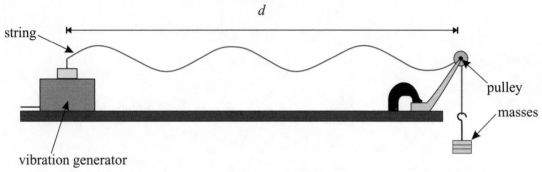

1.1 How many wavelengths are shown on the string in **Figure 1**?

Number of wavelengths = ...
[1]

1.2 The student measures the distance, *d*, shown on **Figure 1**.

Explain how the student can use this measurement to find the wavelength of the wave.

....

....
[1]

[Total 2 marks]

2 A student is investigating water waves in a ripple tank. She sets up the equipment shown in **Figure 2**.

Figure 2

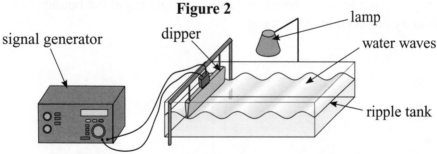

Explain how the student could use this equipment to find the speed of the water waves.

....

....

....

....

....

....
[Total 4 marks]

Topic P6 — Waves

Refraction

1 **Figure 1** shows a ray of light refracting as it passes into a glass block.

Figure 1

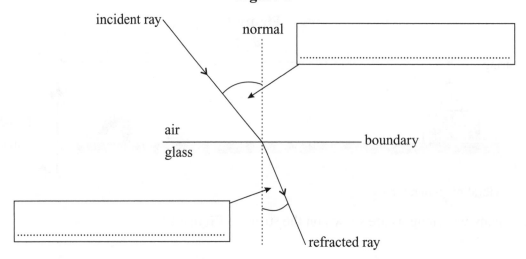

1.1 Label the angle of incidence and the angle of refraction on **Figure 1**.

[1]

1.2 Give the angle between the normal and the boundary.

Angle = ... °
[1]

[Total 2 marks]

2 A light ray travelling through air hits the boundary of a clear plastic block. The angle of incidence at the air to plastic boundary is 30°. The angle of refraction is 20°.

Draw a ray diagram to show the refraction of the light ray at the boundary. The boundary has been drawn for you.

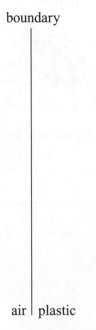

[Total 4 marks]

Electromagnetic Waves

1 All electromagnetic waves are part of the electromagnetic spectrum. **(Grade 1-3)**

Which of the following electromagnetic waves has the highest frequency?
Tick **one** box.

infrared radiation ☐

visible light ☐

gamma rays ☐

ultraviolet radiation ☐

[Total 1 mark]

2 **Table 1** shows the electromagnetic spectrum. It is incomplete. **(Grade 4-5)**

2.1 Complete **Table 1** by filling in the missing types of electromagnetic waves.

[2]

Table 1

Radio Waves	....	Infrared	Visible Light	Ultraviolet	....	Gamma Rays

2.2 Draw an arrow beneath **Table 1** that points from the electromagnetic waves with the shortest wavelength towards the electromagnetic waves with the longest wavelength.

[1]

2.3 Use phrases from the box below to complete the following sentences.

a vacuum	glass	sound	longitudinal	transverse	water

All waves in the electromagnetic spectrum are .... waves.

All electromagnetic waves travel at the same speed in ....

[2]

2.4 Changes in atoms can create different types of electromagnetic waves.
What type of electromagnetic wave is generated by changes in the nucleus of an atom?

....

[1]

[Total 6 marks]

Exam Practice Tip

You need to know each type of electromagnetic radiation in the EM spectrum for your exam. You also need to be able to put them in order of increasing frequency or wavelength. Remember, visible light is in the middle of the EM spectrum.

Uses of EM Waves

The phrases below show parts of a passage describing the uses of radio waves. Number each phrase 1 to 5 to show the correct order of parts. The first one has been done for you.

☐ ...can send signals very long distances.

1 Radio waves can be used to...

☐ ...transmit TV signals...

☐ ...and radio signals.

☐ Some wavelengths...

---

1 Microwave radiation can be used to cook food. **Grade 3-4**

1.1 Use words from the box below to complete the sentences.

emits	reflects	increase	absorbs	decrease

When food is cooked in a microwave oven, water in the food .... microwaves.

This causes the temperature of the food to ....

[2]

1.2 Give **one** other use of microwave radiation.

....

[1]

[Total 3 marks]

---

2 Infrared cameras are used to create images of objects in the dark.
They work by detecting the amount of infrared radiation given out by an object. **Grade 3-4**

2.1 Which phrase, **A**, **B** or **C**, should be used to complete the sentence below?
Write the correct letter, **A**, **B** or **C**, in the space below.

A more infrared radiation than

B the same amount of infrared radiation as

C less infrared radiation than

Hotter objects give out .... cooler objects.

[1]

2.2 Give **two** other devices that use infrared radiation.

1. ....

2. ....

[2]

[Total 3 marks]

More Uses of EM Waves

1 Visible light and ultraviolet radiation are parts of the electromagnetic spectrum. **Grade 1-3**

1.1 Which of the following is a use of visible light? Tick **one** box.

fibre-optic cables for communication ☐

suntanning lamps ☐

cooking food ☐

[1]

1.2 Which of the following is a use of ultraviolet light? Tick **one** box.

cooking food ☐

communicating by satellite ☐

energy efficient lamps ☐

sending TV signals ☐

[1]

1.3 Name **one** other use of ultraviolet light.

....

[1]

[Total 3 marks]

2 Electromagnetic waves can be used to treat illnesses. **Grade 3-4**

2.1 Give **two** types of electromagnetic wave that can be used to treat cancer

1. ....

2. ....

[2]

2.2 Describe **one** other use of an electromagnetic wave in medicine.

....

....

[1]

[Total 3 marks]

Exam Practice Tip

Electromagnetic radiation has a lot of uses. Make sure you know at least one use for each part of the EM spectrum. Being able to remember the different uses is an easy way to get yourself some marks in the exam.

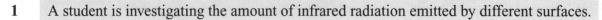

PRACTICAL # Investigating IR Radiation

1 A student is investigating the amount of infrared radiation emitted by different surfaces.

The equipment the student uses is shown in **Figure 1**.

She uses a Leslie cube with four different surfaces.

The student places an infrared detector in front of each face of the Leslie cube.
Each detector is placed the same distance from the cube.

Figure 1

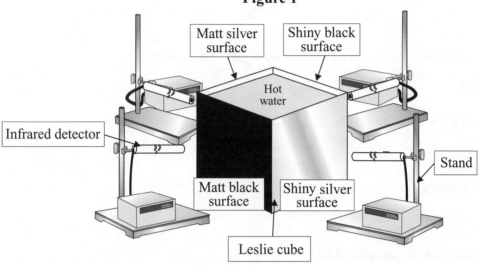

The student recorded how much radiation was detected by each infrared detector.
Her results are shown in **Table 1**.

Table 1

	Matt silver surface	Shiny silver surface	Matt black surface	Shiny black surface
Reading on infrared detector	63	45	90	74

1.1 Suggest a suitable graph or chart the student could use to present their results.
Give a reason for your answer.

Suggestion ....

Reason ....

....

[2]

1.2 Use the information in **Table 1** to place the surfaces in order
from the best to worst emitter of infrared radiation.

Best emitter ....

....

....

Worst emitter ....

[1]

[Total 3 marks]

Topic P6 — Waves

Investigating IR Absorption PRACTICAL

1* A student is investigating how well different surfaces absorb infrared radiation.

Grade
4-5

The student has the equipment shown in **Figure 1**.

The silver plates are identical apart from one surface.
One plate has a shiny silver surface, the other plate has a matt black surface.
Both plates have a small metal ball stuck to a shiny silver side with wax.

Figure 1

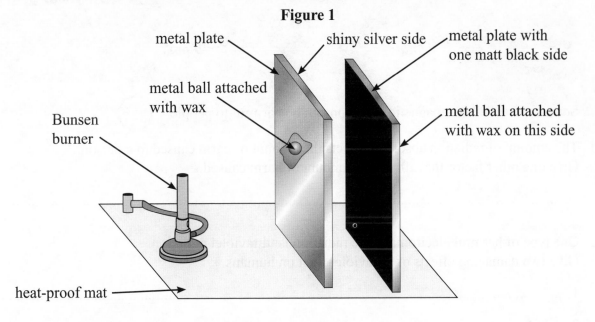

metal plate   shiny silver side   metal plate with one matt black side

metal ball attached with wax   metal ball attached with wax on this side

Bunsen burner

heat-proof mat

The student wants to find out whether the shiny silver or matt black surface is better at absorbing infrared radiation.

Describe an experiment the student could carry out to investigate this using the equipment in **Figure 1**.

....

....

....

....

....

....

....

....

....

....

....

[Total 6 marks]

Topic P6 — Waves

Dangers of Electromagnetic Waves

Radiation dose is measured in sieverts (Sv). It can also be measured in millisieverts (mSv). Draw a ring around the value below which is equal to 1 Sv.

50 mSv   1000 mSv   1 000 000 mSv

100 mSv   0.001 mSv

1 Some types of electromagnetic radiation can be harmful to people. *(Grade 3-4)*

1.1 The amount of radiation absorbed affects the amount of harm caused to a person.
Give **one** other factor that affects the amount of harm caused.

....

[1]

1.2 One type of harmful electromagnetic radiation is ultraviolet radiation.
Give **two** damaging effects of ultraviolet light on humans.

1. ....

2. ....

[2]

[Total 3 marks]

2* **Table 1** lists the radiation doses for two medical procedures done to a patient. *(Grade 4-5)*

Table 1

Procedure	Typical radiation dose (mSv)
X-ray image of skull	0.07
X-ray image of lower spine	1.4

Compare the risk of harm to the patient from both procedures.
Your answer should include a description of the harmful effects that the patient may experience due to the radiation used in each of these procedures.

....

....

....

....

....

....

[Total 4 marks]

Permanent and Induced Magnets

Warm-Up

Circle the type of force each pair of magnets experiences when brought close together.

| N | S | N | S |

attractive / repulsive

| N | S | S | N |

attractive / repulsive

1 Which of the following is always true for a permanent magnet and a magnetic material? Tick **one** box.

Grade 1-3

the force between them is always repulsive ☐

the force between them is always attractive ☐

the force between them can be either attractive or repulsive ☐

[Total 1 mark]

2 The passage below describes magnetic forces. Use words from the box below to complete the passage.

Grade 3-4

| strongest | north | non-contact | weakest | south | contact |

Magnetic forces are examples of .... forces. The direction of the magnetic

field shows the direction that the force would act on a .... pole at that point.

The field is .... at the poles of the magnet.

[Total 3 marks]

3 **Figure 1** shows two bars of metal. One is a permanent magnet. One is made from a magnetic metal. The magnetic field pattern around the bars is shown.

Grade 4-5

Permanent bar magnet

Figure 1

Magnetic material

| N | S |

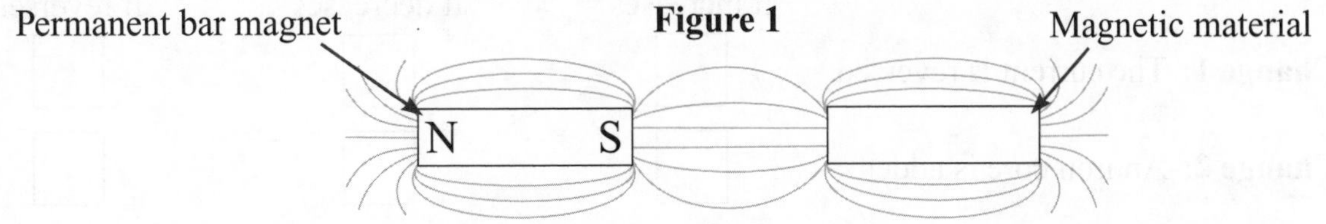

3.1 Explain why there is a magnetic field pattern around the magnetic material.

....

....

[2]

3.2 Suggest what the magnetic material might be.

....

[1]

[Total 3 marks]

Electromagnetism

1 **Figure 1** shows a current-carrying wire and the magnetic field pattern around it. Three points are labelled **X**, **Y** and **Z**.

Grade 4-5

Figure 1

1.1 Draw an arrow on each magnetic field line to show its direction.

[1]

magnetic field lines — wire

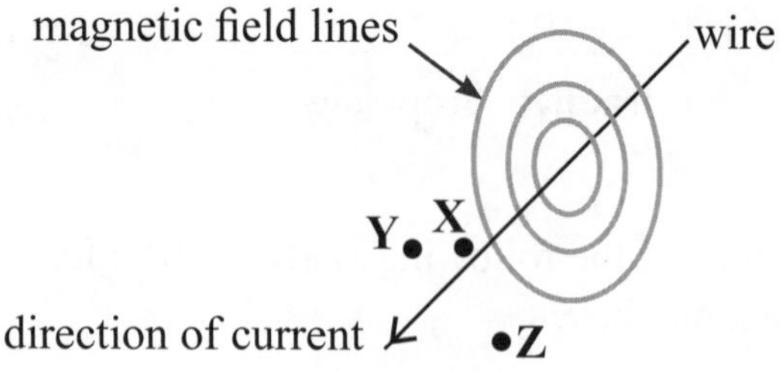

1.2 State at which point, **X**, **Y** or **Z**, the magnetic field is strongest.

....
[1]

Y. **X**

direction of current

•Z

1.3 The wire above is carrying a current of 0.5 A. A second wire is carrying a current of 0.2 A. Explain which wire has the strongest magnetic field around it.

....

....

[2]

[Total 4 marks]

2 **Figure 2** shows a solenoid carrying a current. A magnetic field is produced inside and around the solenoid.

Grade 4-5

Figure 2

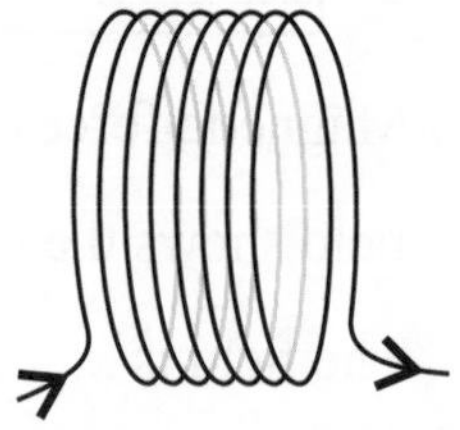

2.1 Describe the magnetic field produced inside the solenoid.

....

....
[2]

2.2 The two changes listed below are made to the solenoid. What happens to the magnetic field around the solenoid in each case? Tick **one** box for each change.

	It increases	It decreases	It reverses
Change 1: The current is reversed.	☐	☐	☐
Change 2: An iron core is added.	☐	☐	☐

[2]

2.3 What is the solenoid known as once an iron core has been added?

....

[1]

[Total 5 marks]

> ***Exam Practice Tip***
> A wire with a current flowing through it always has a magnetic field around it, no matter what shape it is bent into. Make sure you know how you can change the strength and the direction of a magnetic field around a wire.

Topic P7 — Magnetism and Electromagnetism

Biology Mixed Questions

1   **Figure 1** shows a type of animal cell.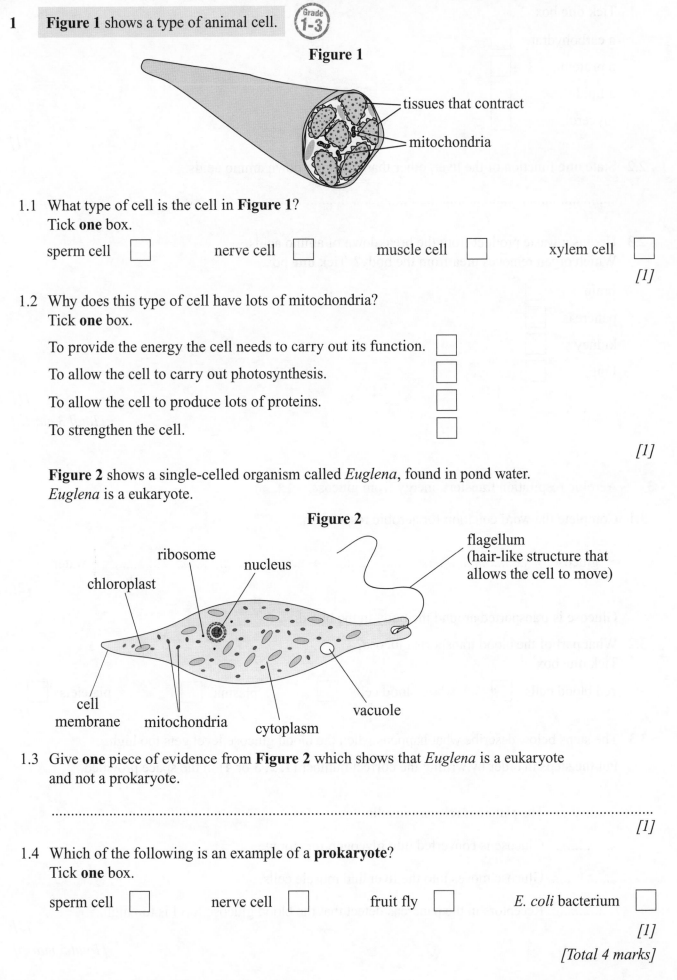

Figure 1

1.1 What type of cell is the cell in **Figure 1**?
     Tick **one** box.

     sperm cell ☐   nerve cell ☐   muscle cell ☐   xylem cell ☐
                                                                                    [1]

1.2 Why does this type of cell have lots of mitochondria?
     Tick **one** box.

     To provide the energy the cell needs to carry out its function. ☐

     To allow the cell to carry out photosynthesis. ☐

     To allow the cell to produce lots of proteins. ☐

     To strengthen the cell. ☐
                                                                                    [1]

Figure 2 shows a single-celled organism called *Euglena*, found in pond water.
Euglena is a eukaryote.

Figure 2

1.3 Give **one** piece of evidence from **Figure 2** which shows that *Euglena* is a eukaryote
     and not a prokaryote.

     ....
                                                                                    [1]

1.4 Which of the following is an example of a **prokaryote**?
     Tick **one** box.

     sperm cell ☐   nerve cell ☐   fruit fly ☐   *E. coli* bacterium ☐
                                                                                    [1]

                                                                      [Total 4 marks]

2 One of the functions of the liver is to break down excess amino acids. (Grade 1-3)

2.1 Which of the following molecules is made up of amino acids?
Tick **one** box.

a carbohydrate ☐

a protein ☐

a lipid ☐

glycerol ☐

[1]

2.2 State **one** function of the liver, other than breaking down amino acids.

....

[1]

2.3 Urea is a waste product from the breakdown of amino acids.
Which organ removes urea from the body? Tick **one** box.

brain ☐

pancreas ☐

kidney ☐

lung ☐

[1]

[Total 3 marks]

3 Aerobic respiration transfers energy from glucose. (Grade 3-4)

3.1 Complete the word equation for aerobic respiration.

glucose + ... → .... + water

[2]

Glucose is transported around the body in the blood.

3.2 What part of the blood transports glucose?
Tick **one** box.

red blood cells ☐   white blood cells ☐   plasma ☐   platelets ☐

[1]

3.3 The steps below describe what happens when the blood glucose level gets too high.

Put the steps in order by writing the correct number (**1**, **2**, **3** or **4**) in the space provided.

.... The pancreas releases insulin.

.... Glucose is converted into glycogen for storage.

.... Glucose moves into the liver and muscle cells.

.... Receptors in the pancreas detect that the blood glucose level is too high.

[2]

[Total 5 marks]

4 **Figure 3** shows a plant cell with one of its subcellular structures magnified. The overall movement of four molecules into and out of the subcellular structure is also shown.

Figure 3

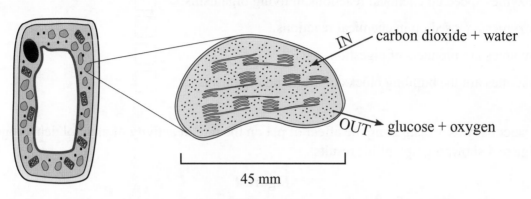

IN — carbon dioxide + water

OUT — glucose + oxygen

45 mm

4.1 Look at the movements of carbon dioxide, water, glucose and oxygen in **Figure 3**.
What reaction do these movements suggest is taking place in the magnified subcellular structure?

....
[1]

4.2 What is the name of the magnified subcellular structure in **Figure 3**?

....
[1]

4.3 The width of the subcellular structure when viewed using a microscope is 45 mm.
What is the width of the magnified image in μm?
Tick **one** box.

45 000 μm ☐

0.045 μm ☐

4500 μm ☐

4.5 μm ☐

[1]

The cell in **Figure 3** is from a leaf.
4.4 Describe how carbon dioxide enters a leaf.

....

....
[2]

4.5 What is the name of the process which transports water up a plant and into the leaves?

....
[1]

4.6 After glucose has been produced by a plant cell, some of it leaves the cell to be transported around the plant. What is the name of the transportation process?

....
[1]

[Total 7 marks]

Biology Mixed Questions

5 Alcohol dehydrogenase enzymes break down alcohol in the body. (Grade 4-5)

5.1 Which of the following sentences about enzymes is correct?
Tick **one** box.

Enzymes speed up chemical reactions in living organisms. ☐

Enzymes are used up in chemical reactions. ☐

Enzymes are products of digestion. ☐

Enzymes are the building blocks of all living organisms. ☐

[1]

A scientist was investigating the effect of pH on the rate of activity of alcohol dehydrogenase. **Figure 4** shows a graph of his results.

Figure 4

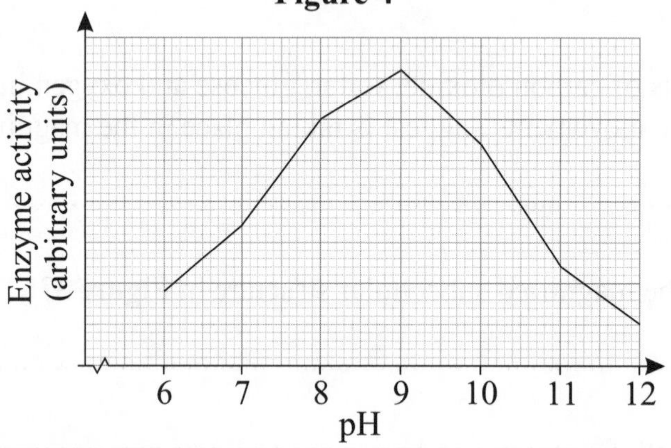

5.2 What is the optimum pH for the enzyme?

....

[1]

5.3 Suggest and explain the effect an acid with a pH of 1 would have on the enzyme.

....

....

....

[3]

5.4 Which of the following statements about alcohol is correct?
Tick **one** box.

Alcohol is a risk factor for several communicable diseases. ☐

Alcohol is a risk factor for lung cancer. ☐

Alcohol can cause liver damage. ☐

Alcohol has no effect on brain function. ☐

[1]

5.5 Alcohol can be produced by yeast cells when they respire.
What type of respiration is involved in the production of alcohol?

....

[1]

[Total 7 marks]

Biology Mixed Questions

6 **Figure 5** shows an example of a grassland food chain.

Figure 5

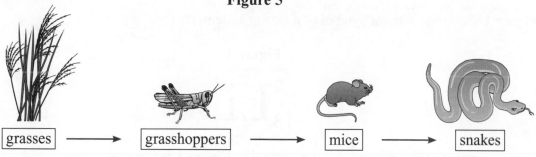

grasses ⟶ grasshoppers ⟶ mice ⟶ snakes

6.1 Grasses are the producer in this food chain.
What is meant by the term producer?

....

....

[1]

6.2 Give **one** biotic factor that may reduce the amount of grass in this food chain.

....

[1]

6.3 Mice are also eaten by owls.
What might happen to the population of **snakes** if owls were introduced into the ecosystem?
Give a reason for your answer.

....

....

....

[2]

A scientist is investigating the grassland ecosystem.

6.4 Describe a method that the scientist could use to investigate whether
the distribution of grasses changes across the ecosystem.

....

....

....

[3]

6.5 The scientist says: "The grassland is a stable community."
What is meant by a stable community?

....

....

....

[2]

[Total 9 marks]

Chemistry Mixed Questions

1   **Figure 1** shows the nuclear symbol of a Group 1 element.   (Grade 1-3)

Figure 1

$$^{7}_{3}\text{Li}$$

1.1   Write the name of the element that the symbol in **Figure 1** represents.

....

[1]

1.2   Name another element in the same group as the element shown in **Figure 1**.

....

[1]

1.3   Atoms contain protons, neutrons and electrons. Draw **one** line from each of these particles to show how many there are in an atom of the element shown in **Figure 1**.

Particle	Number in one atom of Li
proton	3
electron	4
neutron	3

[1]

1.4   The element in **Figure 1** is a metal. Which of the following diagrams shows the structure of a metal? Tick **one** box.

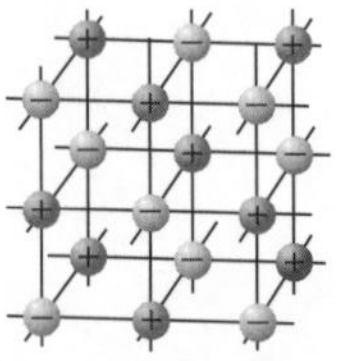

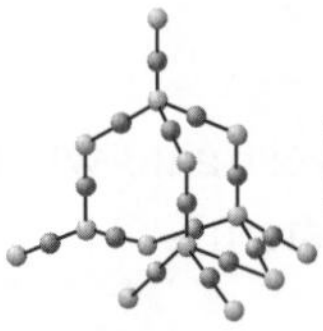

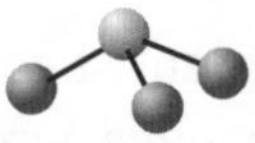

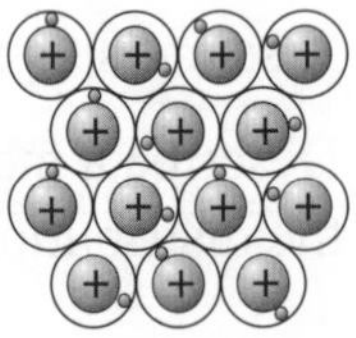

[1]

1.5   The element in **Figure 1** reacts with water. One of the products of this reaction is a gas. When a lit splint is placed in the gas, a squeaky popping noise is made. What gas was produced? Tick **one** box.

Carbon dioxide ☐   Chlorine ☐   Oxygen ☐   Hydrogen ☐

[1]

1.6   LiOH is also produced in the reaction between the element in **Figure 1** and water. Complete the sentence below. Use a word from the box.

oxide	hydroxide	carbonate

When a Group 1 element reacts with water a metal .... is formed.

[1]

[Total 6 marks]

2 Hydrochloric acid and sodium hydroxide react in a neutralisation reaction.

2.1 A student carries out an experiment to find the volume of hydrochloric acid needed to neutralise 25 cm³ of sodium hydroxide. She does the experiment three times. Her results are in **Table 1**.

Complete **Table 1** to show the mean volume of hydrochloric acid needed.

Table 1

Repeat	1	2	3	mean
Volume (cm³)	35.60	35.90	35.75	....

[2]

2.2 Calculate the uncertainty of the mean.
Use the equation: uncertainty = range ÷ 2

Uncertainty = ... cm³

[2]

2.3 The products of the reaction between hydrochloric acid and sodium hydroxide are sodium chloride and water. Complete the equation below to show this reaction.

.... + NaOH → .... + H_2O

[2]

2.4 The student measures the pH of the sodium hydroxide at the start of the experiment. She then measures the pH as the hydrochloric acid is added and the pH at the end of the reaction.

Describe how the pH of the reaction mixture would change during the experiment.

....

....

....

[3]

2.5 **Figure 2** is a dot and cross diagram showing the formation of sodium chloride. Complete the right-hand side of **Figure 2**. You should add any charges and electrons that are needed.

Figure 2

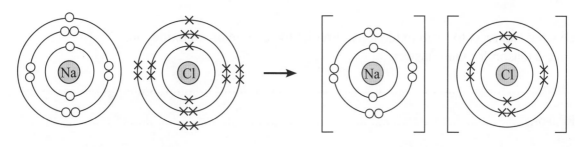

[2]

2.6 State the type of bonding in sodium chloride.

....

[1]

[Total 12 marks]

3 A substance can be classified as an element, a compound or a mixture. (Grade 3-4)

3.1 Draw a line to connect each type of substance with an example of it.

Type of Substance	Example
compound	salt water
element	nitrogen
mixture	iron oxide

[2]

3.2 Calcium carbonate is a compound with the formula $CaCO_3$.
Name the elements that make up calcium carbonate.

....
[2]

3.3 In terms of the substances they contain, what is the difference between pure water and potable water?

....

....
[2]

3.4 Mixtures can be separated by physical methods.
Name **two** techniques that can be used to separate mixtures

1 ....

2 ....
[2]

[Total 8 marks]

4 Oxygen atoms have the electronic structure 2, 6. (Grade 4-5)

4.1 State which group of the periodic table oxygen is in.
Explain your answer with reference to the electronic structure of oxygen.

Group: ....

Explanation: ....
[2]

4.2 Oxygen can react to form oxide ions. Predict the charge on an oxide ion.
Give a reason for your answer.

Charge: ....

Reason: ....
[2]

4.3 When magnesium reacts with oxygen, it forms magnesium oxide.
What type of reaction does magnesium take part in? Tick **one** box.

Displacement ☐   Oxidation ☐   Electrolysis ☐   Reduction ☐
[1]

[Total 5 marks]

5 Alkanes are hydrocarbon compounds found in crude oil. **Table 2** shows how the boiling points of some alkanes change as the molecules get bigger.

Table 2

Alkane	Propane	Butane	Pentane	Hexane	Heptane
Molecular formula	C_3H_8	C_4H_{10}	C_5H_{12}	C_6H_{14}	C_7H_{16}
Boiling point (°C)	−42	−0.5		69	98

5.1 Using the data in **Table 1**, plot a graph of the number of carbon atoms in an alkane molecule against boiling point on the axes below. Draw a smooth curve through the points that you plot.

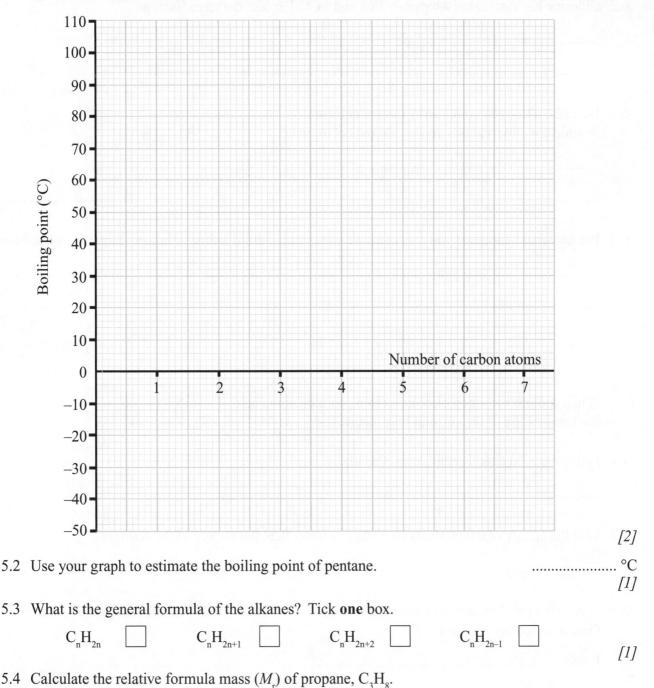

[2]

5.2 Use your graph to estimate the boiling point of pentane. .... °C

[1]

5.3 What is the general formula of the alkanes? Tick **one** box.

C_nH_{2n} ☐ C_nH_{2n+1} ☐ C_nH_{2n+2} ☐ C_nH_{2n-1} ☐

[1]

5.4 Calculate the relative formula mass (M_r) of propane, C_3H_8.
Relative atomic masses (A_r): C = 12, H = 1

Relative formula mass = ...

[1]

[Total 5 marks]

Chemistry Mixed Questions

6 Chlorine is a Group 7 element that exists as molecules of Cl_2.

6.1 Complete the dot-and-cross diagram below to show the bonding in Cl_2.
You only need to show the outer electron shells.

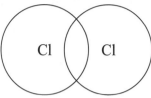

[2]

6.2 Chlorine has two main isotopes — ^{35}Cl and ^{37}Cl. Explain the term 'isotope'.

....

....

[2]

6.3 Describe a test you could carry out for chlorine.
Include any observations you would expect to make.

....

....

[2]

6.4 Predict what happens if you mix chlorine water and sodium iodide solution. Explain your answer.

....

....

[2]

[Total 8 marks]

7 When sodium hydrogen carbonate reacts with ethanoic acid, the temperature of the surroundings decreases.

7.1 Is this reaction endothermic or exothermic?

....

[1]

7.2 Will the energy of the products be higher or lower than the energy of the reactants?

....

[1]

7.3 What effect will increasing the concentration of ethanoic acid have on the rate of the reaction?
Give a reason for your answer.

Effect: ....

Reason: ....

....

[3]

[Total 5 marks]

8 Aluminium and iron can be obtained by extracting them from their ores.
Both metals can also be obtained from recycling aluminium and iron items.

Table 3

Material	Extraction process	Energy saved by recycling
Aluminium	Electrolysis	Around 95%
Iron	Reduction with carbon	Around 60%

8.1 Look at **Table 3**. Suggest whether the extraction of aluminium or iron
will have a larger carbon footprint. Give a reason for your answer.

Extraction process: ....

Reason: ....

....

....

[4]

8.2 **Table 3** shows that energy is saved when aluminium and iron are obtained from recycled metals
rather than being extracted from their ores. Give **two** other advantages of recycling metals.

1 ....

2 ....

[2]

[Total 6 marks]

9* The structure and bonding of substances affects their properties. (Grade 4-5)

Table 4

	Hardness	Melting point	Conducts electricity?
Diamond	Hard	High	No
Graphite	Soft	High	Yes

Explain how the structure and bonding of diamond and graphite
give them the properties listed in **Table 4**.

Your answer should include details of how the atoms are arranged and how they're held together.

....

....

....

....

....

....

....

....

[Total 6 marks]

Physics Mixed Questions

1   The three states of matter are solid, liquid and gas.

1.1   Materials can change state if they are heated or cooled.
Draw **one** line from each change of state to its correct name.

Change of state   **Name**

freezing

solid to liquid

condensing

liquid to solid

melting

[2]

1.2   Use a phrase from the box below to complete the sentence.

as dense as	denser than	less dense than

Gases are usually .... liquids.

[1]

[Total 3 marks]

2   **Figure 1** shows a displacement-distance graph for a sound wave.

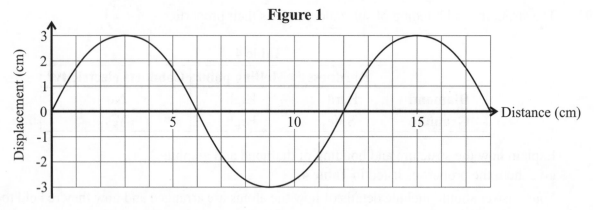

2.1   What is the amplitude of the wave? Tick **one** box.

3 cm   ☐

6 cm   ☐

12 cm   ☐

[1]

2.2   What is the approximate speed of sound in air? Tick **one** box.

3 m/s   ☐

330 m/s   ☐

330 000 m/s ☐

[1]

[Total 2 marks]

3 A cyclist accelerates from rest. (Grade 3-4)

3.1 What is the typical speed of a cyclist? Tick **one** box.

1.5 m/s ☐   3 m/s ☐   6 m/s ☐   14 m/s ☐
[1]

3.2 It takes the cyclist 10 seconds to reach this speed.
Calculate his acceleration during these 10 seconds. Use the equation:

$$\text{acceleration} = \text{change in velocity} \div \text{time taken}$$

Acceleration = ... m/s²
[2]

[Total 3 marks]

4 A student is investigating the relationship between mass and weight. (Grade 3-4)

4.1 Mass is a scalar quantity. Weight is a vector quantity.
Explain what is meant by a scalar quantity.

....
[1]

4.2 Use words from the box below to complete the passage.

weight	kilograms	force	newtons	mass	newton metres

The force on an object due to gravity is called its ....

It is measured in .... You can think of weight as acting from a single

point on an object. This point is called the centre of ....
[3]

4.3 The student measures the mass of her full pencil case.
She then measures its weight.

What piece of equipment could she use to directly measure the weight of the pencil case?
Tick **one** box.

mass balance ☐

thermometer ☐

newtonmeter ☐

measuring cylinder ☐
[1]

4.4 The student states that the object would weigh the same on a planet with a smaller gravitational
field strength. Is she correct? Explain your answer.

....

....
[1]

[Total 6 marks]

Physics Mixed Questions

5 A girl walks her dog.
She records the total distance she has travelled every 5 minutes.

5.1 She uses the information she collects to draw a distance-time graph for her walk.
State what quantity the gradient of a distance-time graph gives.

....

[1]

5.2 She walked a distance of 420 m in 5.0 minutes.
Calculate the average speed at which she walked.
Use the equation:

$$\text{speed} = \text{distance travelled} \div \text{time}$$

Speed = ... m/s

[3]

5.3 Whilst walking, the girl throws a ball for her dog to chase.
Each time she throws the ball, she transfers energy to the ball's kinetic energy store.
How is energy transferred to the ball? Tick **one** box.

electrically ☐

mechanically ☐

by heating ☐

by radiation ☐

[1]

[Total 5 marks]

6 Gamma rays are a type of electromagnetic wave.

6.1 State **one** use of gamma rays.

....

[1]

6.2 The equation shows a nucleus emitting a gamma ray.
Determine the values of A and B.

$$^{99}_{43}\text{Tc} \rightarrow \, ^{A}_{43}\text{Tc} + \, ^{B}_{0}\gamma$$

A = ...

B = ...

[2]

6.3 A scientist works with gamma radiation. He uses a shield to protect himself from being irradiated by gamma rays. Suggest what material this shield is made from.

....

[1]

[Total 4 marks]

PRACTICAL

7   A student tests the relationship between the potential
difference across a diode and the current through it.

7.1   Which of the following shows an *I-V* graph for a diode? Tick **one** box.

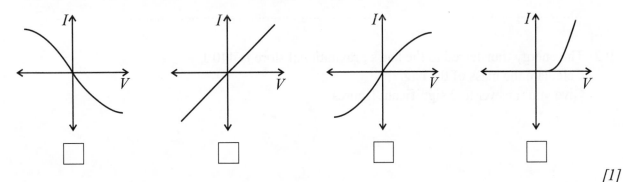

[1]

When the potential difference across the diode is 2.4 V, the current through the diode is 0.4 A.

7.2   Write down the equation that links potential difference, current and resistance.

....

[1]

7.3   Calculate the resistance of the diode.

Resistance = ... Ω

[3]

[Total 5 marks]

---

8   Two beakers containing 0.5 kg of water are at room temperature. A student
heats the water using two different electric heaters. You can assume both heaters
are 100% efficient. Heater A takes 340 s to heat the water in one of the beakers
to 100 °C. Heater B takes 170 s to heat the water in the other beaker to 100 °C.

8.1   In terms of energy transfer, which heater is more powerful, Heater A or Heater B?
Explain your answer.

....

....

[2]

8.2   Heater A is used to heat 0.5 kg of water from 20 °C to 50 °C.
The specific heat capacity of water is 4200 J/kg °C.
Calculate the energy transferred to the water.
Use an equation from the Equations List.

Energy = ... J

[3]

[Total 5 marks]

Physics Mixed Questions

9   A student carries a bag of magnets to a classroom.   (Grade 4-5)

The change in height of the bag is 9.0 m.   The Earth's gravitational field strength is 9.8 N/kg.

9.1   Write down the equation which links energy in a gravitational potential energy store, mass, gravitational field strength and height.

....

[1]

9.2   The energy transferred to the bag's gravitational store is 440 J.
Calculate the mass of the bag.
Give your answer to 2 significant figures.

Mass = ... kg
[3]

9.3   The student wants to investigate the magnetic field produced by one of the magnets from the bag.   She decides to use a compass to plot the magnetic field.
Figure 2 shows a bar magnet.
Draw the magnetic field lines around the magnet in **Figure 2**.

Figure 2

N   S

[2]

9.4   When the student moves the compass away from the magnet, the needle points north.   Explain why this happens.

....

....

....

[2]

9.5   Describe the difference between a permanent and an induced magnet.

....

....

[2]

[Total 10 marks]

10 A child is playing with a remote-controlled toy car.
The car is travelling at a constant speed.

Figure 3

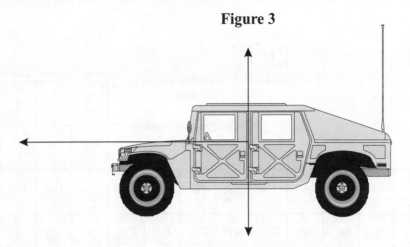

10.1 **Figure 3** shows an incomplete force diagram for the toy.
Complete the force diagram by drawing the missing resistive force acting on the car.

[2]

10.2 Write down the equation that links energy in a kinetic energy store, mass and speed.

....

[1]

10.3 The car travels at 5.0 m/s. The car has 7.5 J of energy in its kinetic energy store.
Calculate the mass of the car.

Mass = ... kg

[3]

10.4 The car's battery runs out of power and the car rolls up a hill and stops at the top.
Describe the energy transfers that take place after the battery stops working.

....

....

....

[2]

10.5 The car is powered by an electric motor. The efficiency of the motor is 0.65.
The total input energy transfer is 700 J.

Calculate the energy wasted by the motor.

Wasted energy = ... J

[3]

[Total 11 marks]

The Periodic Table

Periods

Group 0

						1 H Hydrogen 1											4 He Helium 2

Group 1   Group 2

Relative atomic mass

Atomic (proton) number

Group 3 Group 4 Group 5 Group 6 Group 7

Period	Group 1	Group 2										Group 3	Group 4	Group 5	Group 6	Group 7	Group 0
2	7 Li Lithium 3	9 Be Beryllium 4										11 B Boron 5	12 C Carbon 6	14 N Nitrogen 7	16 O Oxygen 8	19 F Fluorine 9	20 Ne Neon 10
3	23 Na Sodium 11	24 Mg Magnesium 12										27 Al Aluminium 13	28 Si Silicon 14	31 P Phosphorus 15	32 S Sulfur 16	35.5 Cl Chlorine 17	40 Ar Argon 18
4	39 K Potassium 19	40 Ca Calcium 20	45 Sc Scandium 21	48 Ti Titanium 22	51 V Vanadium 23	52 Cr Chromium 24	55 Mn Manganese 25	56 Fe Iron 26	59 Co Cobalt 27	59 Ni Nickel 28	63.5 Cu Copper 29	65 Zn Zinc 30	70 Ga Gallium 31	73 Ge Germanium 32	75 As Arsenic 33	79 Se Selenium 34	80 Br Bromine 35	84 Kr Krypton 36

5	85 Rb Rubidium 37	88 Sr Strontium 38	89 Y Yttrium 39	91 Zr Zirconium 40	93 Nb Niobium 41	96 Mo Molybdenum 42	98 Tc Technetium 43	101 Ru Ruthenium 44	103 Rh Rhodium 45	106 Pd Palladium 46	108 Ag Silver 47	112 Cd Cadmium 48	115 In Indium 49	119 Sn Tin 50	122 Sb Antimony 51	128 Te Tellurium 52	127 I Iodine 53	131 Xe Xenon 54
6	133 Cs Caesium 55	137 Ba Barium 56	139 La Lanthanum 57	178 Hf Hafnium 72	181 Ta Tantalum 73	184 W Tungsten 74	186 Re Rhenium 75	190 Os Osmium 76	192 Ir Iridium 77	195 Pt Platinum 78	197 Au Gold 79	201 Hg Mercury 80	204 Tl Thallium 81	207 Pb Lead 82	209 Bi Bismuth 83	[209] Po Polonium 84	[210] At Astatine 85	[222] Rn Radon 86
7	[223] Fr Francium 87	[226] Ra Radium 88	[227] Ac Actinium 89	[261] Rf Rutherfordium 104	[262] Db Dubnium 105	[266] Sg Seaborgium 106	[264] Bh Bohrium 107	[277] Hs Hassium 108	[268] Mt Meitnerium 109	[271] Ds Darmstadtium 110	[272] Rg Roentgenium 111	[285] Cn Copernicium 112	[286] Uut Ununtrium 113	[289] Fl Flerovium 114	[289] Uup Ununpentium 115	[293] Lv Livermorium 116	[294] Uus Ununseptium 117	[294] Uuo Ununoctium 118

The Lanthanides (atomic numbers 58-71) and the Actinides (atomic numbers 90-103) are not shown in this table.

Physics Equations List

Topic P1 — Energy

$E_e = \frac{1}{2}ke^2$	elastic potential energy = 0.5 × spring constant × (extension)^2
$\Delta E = mc\Delta\theta$	change in thermal energy = mass × specific heat capacity × temperature change
$E = mL$	thermal energy for a change of state = mass × specific latent heat

Topic P5 — Forces

$v^2 - u^2 = 2as$	(final velocity)^2 − (initial velocity)^2 = 2 × acceleration × distance

Topic P6 — Waves

$$\text{period} = \frac{1}{\text{frequency}}$$